How Networks Work

4th Edition

Frank J. Derfler, Jr., and Les Freed

Illustrated by Michael Troller, Steve Adams, and Patricia Douglas

Que Corporation
An imprint of Macmillan Computer Publishing USA
Indianapolis, Indiana

How Networks Work, 4th Edition

By Frank J. Derfler, Jr., and Les Reed

How Networks Work, 4th Edition © 1998 by Macmillan Computer Publishing/Que Corporation

Library of Congress Catalog No.: 98-85230

ISBN: 0-7897-1595-3

01 00 99 98   4 3 2 1

Interpretation of the printing code: the rightmost double-digit number is the year of the book's printing; the rightmost single-digit number, the number of the book's printing. For example, a printing code of 98-1 shows that the first printing of the book occurred in 1998.

Screen reproductions in this book were created by using Collage Plus from Inner Media, Inc., Hollis, NH.

This book was produced digitally by Macmillan Computer Publishing and manufactured using computer-to-plate technology (a film-less process) by GAC/Shepard Poorman, Indianapolis, Indiana.

Executive Editor	Laurie Petrycki
Development Editor	Jim Chalex
Managing Editor	Sarah Kearns
Project Editor	Mike La Bonne
Indexer	Chris Barrick
Technical Editor	Wade Ellery
Technical Illustrators	Steve Adams, Patricia Douglas
Production Team	Jeanne Clark, John Etchison, Trina Wurst

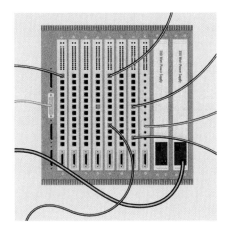

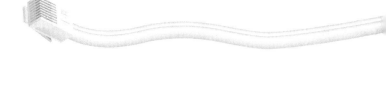

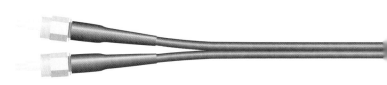

MORE than 80 percent of the personal computers used in business and education are connected to a network or the Internet. The chances are good that you'll have to interact with a network soon if you don't already. This book helps you understand computer networks in several ways. It helps to scratch the intellectual itch you might have about where the data resides and what goes on inside the cable, equipment, and software. If you understand the basic structure and operation of a network, you can be more efficient in your job. The information in this book is an excellent foundation for growth if you want to learn more about networking. Finally, you can use this book as a training tool for working on networked computers.

Computer networking didn't just emerge as a unique and independent technology. Networking depends on many things you've seen or are familiar with already. In fact, modern networks have roots in the early telegraph and telephone systems. In this book, we take advantage of those historical ties to explain and illustrate the underlying technology of networks in a simple graphic format.

Then, we move into modern networking and explain the relationships between the hardware and software in networks. Our illustrations detail packets, network interface cards, servers, routers, management software, and many other aspects of networking. Our constant goal is to provide useful information in an easily understood manner.

The information in this book isn't specific to any particular type of computer or network operating system. We illustrate models of operation and tell you how some popular products fit into the models. If your computer is an IBM PC, DEC VAX, or an Apple Macintosh; if your network operating system is NetWare, LANtastic, or UNIX; and if your cabling is copper or fiber optic, the information in this book applies to your network.

P A R T

COMMUNICATING BY WIRE

WE—being the modern, up-to-the-minute kind of people computer users tend to be—like to think of networking as something new. Although the art and science of connecting computers via network cable are fairly new, the essential concepts used in computer networks are relatively old—nineteenth-century old, as a matter of fact. The modern-day computer industry owes its existence to three Victorian-era inventions: the telegraph, telephone, and teletypewriter.

Samuel F. B. Morse (father of the telegraph and Morse code) wouldn't recognize a computer if you dropped one on his big toe, but he would recognize the logic and simplicity of ASCII, the essential modern-day computer alphabet and a descendant of Morse's telegraph code. Morse's original telegraph sent data (in the form of letters and numbers) from one place to another by using a series of timed on-and-off pulses of electricity. Today's data communication systems still use on-and-off pulses of electricity to convey information—they just do it much faster than Morse ever imagined possible. In many ways, the telegraph was the first digital data communications system.

Alexander Graham Bell, also, wouldn't know what a modem is, but he would recognize the Victorian-era telephone-line interface that still connects most telephones and modems to the phone company's central office. The worldwide telephone system has changed rapidly over the years (largely due to the use of computers), but the *subscriber loop*—the wire between your home or office and the telephone company's equipment—hasn't changed much since Bell's day. The subscriber loop is an old-fashioned analog audio line. As we'll see, inventors over the years have gone to great lengths to connect digital computer systems to analog telephone lines.

Emile Baudot's invention didn't make his name a household word like Bell's and Morse's, but his multiplex printing telegraph was the forerunner of the computer printer and computer terminal. Other inventors improved and expanded on Baudot's ideas, and the teletypewriter was born. Before the invention of the computer, teletypewriters formed the basis of the Associated Press and United Press International news services. You may never have seen a teletypewriter, but you've probably heard its familiar *chunk-chunk-chunk* rhythm as the background noise on a radio or television newscast. Teletypewriters also form the basis of the worldwide TELEX network—a loosely bound network of machines that allows users to send printed messages to one another. (Although it was one of the most reliable of Teletype Corporation's machines, an ASR-33 Teletype machine played the part of the bad guy in the movie *Fail Safe*. The short version of the otherwise very complicated plot is that the United States and the former Soviet Union engage in nuclear warfare due to the failure of an ASR-33 at the American command headquarters. New York and Moscow are pulverized—all thanks to an errant scrap of paper stuck inside the machine.)

In the following three chapters, we'll show you how these three essential technologies converged to spark the beginning of the computer age.

CHAPTER

1

The Telegraph

ON May 24, 1844, American artist and inventor Samuel Morse sat at a desk in the Supreme Court chamber of the U.S. Capitol building in Washington, D.C., and sent his famous telegraph message—"What hath God wrought"—to a receiver 37 miles away in Baltimore. Morse had spent 12 years and every penny he owned to develop the telegraph.

To give credit where it is due, several other inventors in the United States and Europe also contributed to the development of the telegraph. Two English electrical pioneers, William Cooke and Charles Wheatstone, patented a telegraph in 1845. The Cooke-Wheatstone system was widely used by the British railroad system to relay traffic information between train stations.

The Cooke-Wheatstone telegraph used six wires and a delicate receiver mechanism with five magnetic needles. It was costly to build and cantankerous to operate. Morse's simpler telegraph used only one wire and a less complex, relatively rugged mechanism.

Fortunately for Morse, his telegraph was just what the young United States needed. America was expanding to the West, and Morse's telegraph followed the train tracks westward. Morse assigned his patents to the Magnetic Telegraph Company, and Magnetic signed up licensees to use the Morse patents. By 1851, there were 50 telegraph companies operating hundreds of telegraph offices—most of them located at railroad stations. You can still see old telegraph lines along the rail beds in many parts of the United States. In 1851, the Western Union Company was formed by the merger of 12 smaller telegraph companies. By 1866, Western Union boasted more than 4,000 offices nationwide, making it the world's first communications giant. By the turn of the century, Western Union operated over one million miles of telegraph lines, including two transatlantic cables.

The telegraph seems incredibly simple by today's standards, but it provided a much-needed link between the established business world of the Eastern United States and the sprawling frontier of the West. In one of those pleasant coincidences of history, it was just the right thing at just the right time.

The Telegraph

The telegraph is basically an electromagnet connected to a battery via a switch. When the switch (the Morse key, or telegraph key) is down, current flows from the battery (at the sender's end of the line) through the key, down the wire, and into the sounder at the distant end of the line. By itself, the telegraph can express only two states, on or off. But by varying the timing and spacing of the on-and-off pulses, telegraph operators can send all the letters of the alphabet as well as numbers and punctuation marks. Morse code defines the timing and spacing of each character in terms of long and short "on" states called dashes and dots. For example, the letter A is dot-dash; the letter B is dash-dot-dot-dot.

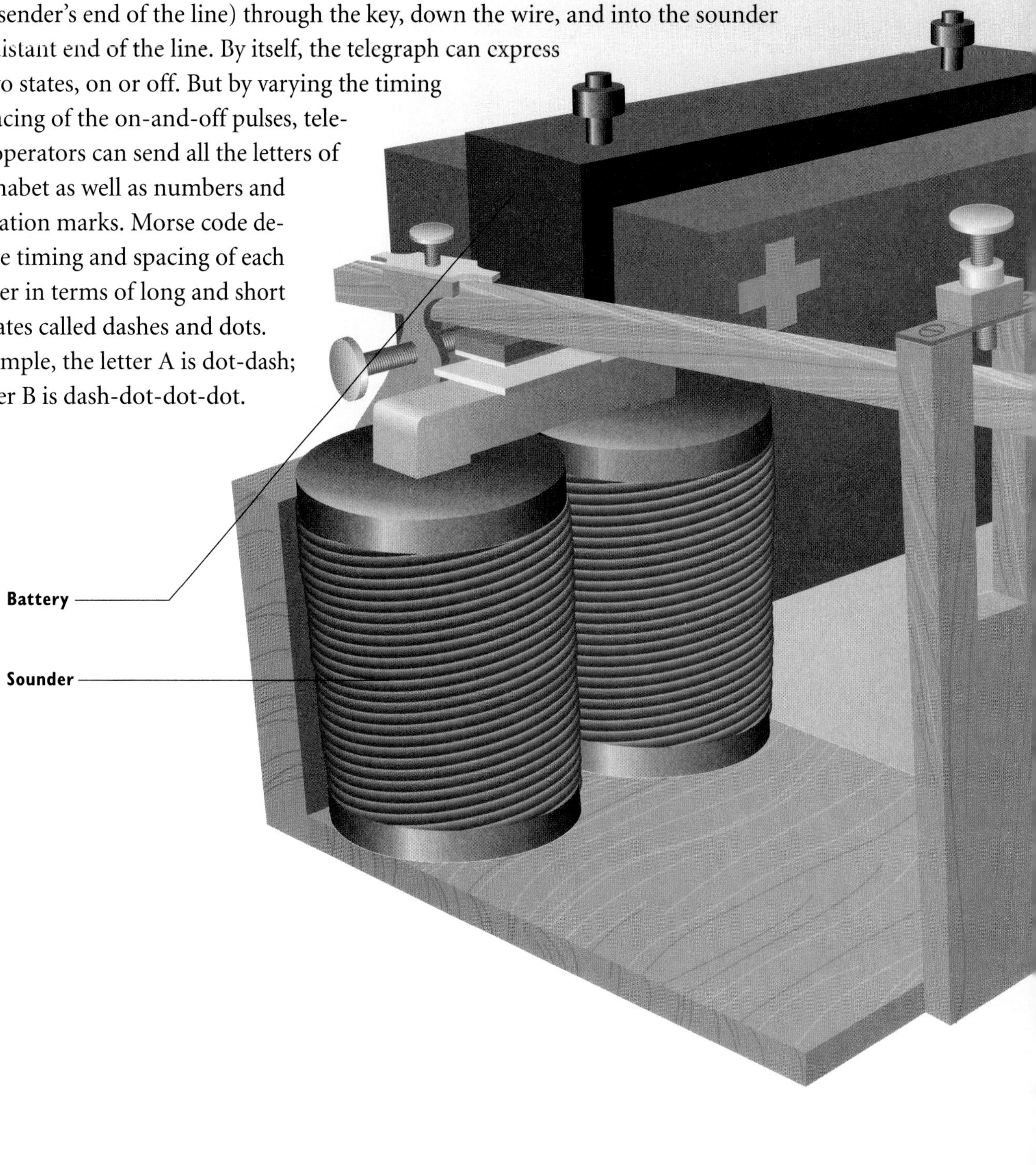

Battery

Sounder

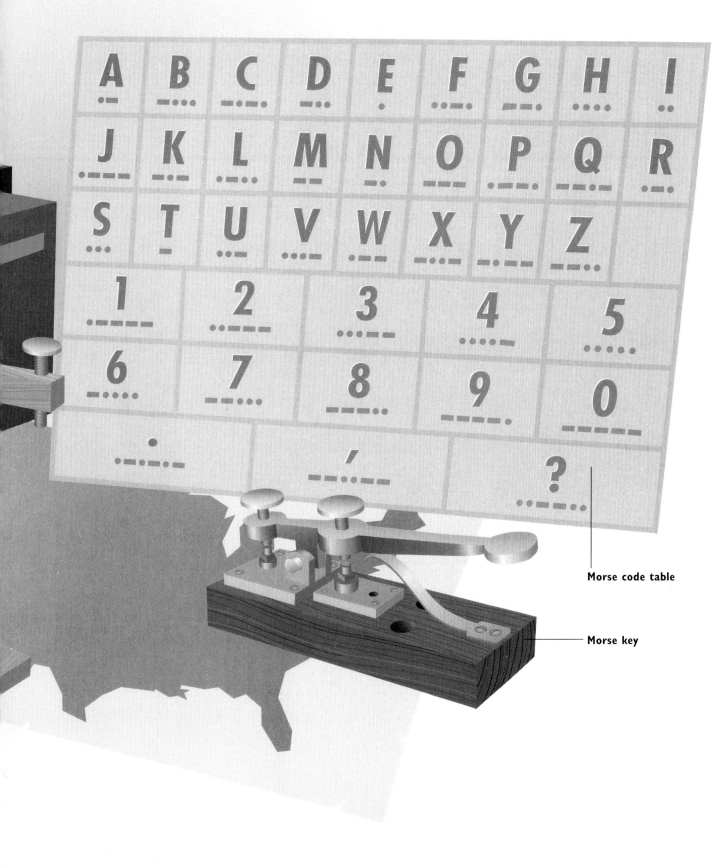

Morse code table

Morse key

The Telegraph

Morse's Port-Rule Telegraph

Morse's original telegraph used an automatic key to send messages and a printing mechanism to print the dots and dashes it received on a long strip of paper. To compose a message, the telegraph operator placed metal pieces in the notched stick, called a *port-rule*. To send the message, the operator placed the port-rule in the sender and turned the crank, moving the port-rule down the track. As the port-rule moved, it touched a metal contact, making or breaking the electrical connection.

At the receiving end, the current from the telegraph line moved an electromagnet up and down. A pencil attached to the magnet drew dots and dashes on a moving strip of paper; the paper was powered by a clock mechanism.

To read the message, the operator deciphered the dots and dashes and transcribed them by hand. Different combinations of dots and dashes represented different words, as defined in a master codebook. The limited number of possible combinations limited the number of words that could be sent. Morse later abandoned the printing mechanism when he discovered that telegraph operators could decipher the dots and dashes by ear.

TO LIGHT THE ENTIRE CAPITOL AND THE SURROUNDING AREAS FOR ALMOST TEN MILES WHEN COMPLETED

Edison's Printing Telegraph

Several famous inventors—including Alexander Bell and Thomas Edison—got their start in the telegraph industry. Edison, who worked as a telegraph operator in his youth, devised a printing telegraph that was used to relay stock-market information to investors. Rather than retaining patent rights, Edison often sold his patent rights to finance research in other areas.

CHAPTER

2

The Telephone

ALEXANDER Graham Bell invented the telephone, right? Well, right and wrong. Although Bell has received the lion's share of the credit, several other inventors also played major roles in the development of the telephone.

In 1861, German schoolteacher Phillip Reis created a device he called a telephone. Reis's device could transmit musical tones; had Reis spent more time refining the equipment, he might have succeeded in producing a viable voice telephone.

The two men who actually did invent the telephone did so under strikingly similar circumstances. Alexander Graham Bell of Boston and Elisha Gray of Chicago were both attempting to invent the *harmonic telegraph*, a device that would allow several telegraph signals to share one telegraph line (a problem later solved by no less an inventor than Thomas Edison). Neither inventor ever produced a working harmonic telegraph, and both men made the jump from telegraph to telephone at about the same time. Both men filed their patent papers with the U.S. Patent Office on the exact same day—February 14, 1876—but Bell arrived a few hours ahead of Gray.

The patent issued to Bell, U.S. Patent Number 174,465, is likely the most valuable patent ever issued. Bell and his backers immediately turned their attention from developing the telephone itself to perfecting and selling their invention.

The early years were not kind to Bell and company, and in early 1877 the Bell organization offered Western Union all rights to the Bell patents for $100,000. Western Union declined, setting off a series of encounters between the two companies that would finally culminate in AT&T's purchase of the remains of Western Union over a hundred years later.

Unimpressed with Bell's telephone, Western Union enlisted the services of Elisha Gray and Thomas Edison to design and market a technically superior telephone. Western Union was a giant corporation and had vast resources to spend on a legal battle. All the Bell Company had were its patents.

Western Union began to set up a telephone system to compete with Bell's. The Bell company filed suit. After two years of legal combat, Western Union's lawyers recommended that the company reach a settlement with Bell. The essential fact was that Bell had, indeed, beaten Gray to the patent office, and it was Bell and not Gray who held the basic telephone patents.

Under the terms of the agreement, Western Union surrendered its rights and patents in the telephone business to Bell. In addition, Western Union turned over its network of telephones to the Bell company in return for 20 percent of rental receipts for the life of the Bell patents.

The legal victory gave Bell a monopoly on the telephone business in the United States. One hundred years later, Bell's company (later known as AT&T) was the largest company in the world. Before the court-ordered dismantling of the AT&T empire in 1984, the company employed over one million people and operated over 100 million telephones.

Early Advances in Telephone Technology

Bell Liquid Telephone Transmitter

All telephones consist of a transmitter (the mouthpiece) and a receiver (the earpiece). To create a working telephone, Bell and the other inventors had to invent those two critical pieces.

Bell pursued two separate designs for the telephone transmitter. His first design used a membrane attached to a metal rod. The metal rod reached down into a cup of mild acid. As the user spoke downward into the microphone, the sound caused the membrane to move, which in turn moved the rod up and down in the cup of acid. As the rod moved up and down, the electrical resistance between the rod and the base of the cup varied.

There were several drawbacks to this variable-resistance, or liquid telephone, transmitter, not least of which was requiring the user to keep a supply of acid on hand. It was the acid, in fact, that caused Bell to utter the famous, "Mr. Watson, come here!"—Bell had spilled the acid on his trousers.

Bell Induction Telephone Transmitter

Bell's second telephone transmitter used the principle of magnetic induction to change sound into electricity. Instead of a cup of acid, the induction transmitter used a membrane attached to a rod surrounded by a coil of wire. Sound striking the membrane moved the rod; as the rod moved back and forth inside the coil, it produced a weak electric current. The advantage of this device was that, theoretically, it could be used as both a transmitter and a receiver. But because the current it produced was very weak, it wasn't successful as a transmitter.

Despite its failure as a transmitter, the induction telephone worked very well as a receiver—so well, in fact, that most modern-day telephones and audio speakers still use a variation on Bell's original design.

Edison's Carbon Transmitter

The first truly practical telephone transmitter was designed by Thomas Edison, under contract for Western Union. Edison had discovered that certain carbon compounds change their electrical resistance when subjected to varying pressure. Edison sandwiched a carbon button between a metal membrane and a metal support. When sound struck the membrane, it exerted pressure on the carbon button, varying the flow of electricity through the microphone.

Despite the hostilities between Bell and Western Union, the Bell people were quick to realize the superiority of Edison's design. When the *Bell v. Western Union* lawsuit was settled in 1879, Bell took over rights to Edison's transmitter. It became the standard telephone transmitter and is still in use today.

Strowger's Dial Telephone

As the telephone grew in popularity, the operator-and-switchboard approach became woefully inadequate. In 1889, a Kansas City undertaker named Almon Brown Strowger took the first step toward automating the phone system. His inventions, the Strowger switch and the telephone dial, allowed a caller to dial the desired number, eliminating the need for an operator.

CHAPTER

3

Printing Telegraphs

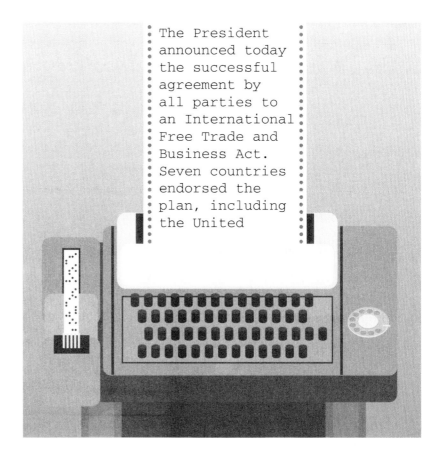

The President announced today the successful agreement by all parties to an International Free Trade and Business Act. Seven countries endorsed the plan, including the United

MORSE'S telegraph opened up the frontiers of electronic communications, but it had many shortcomings. First and foremost, the original Morse design allowed for only one conversation on the line at one time. Wire was handmade then, brittle, and very expensive. Installing the wire along the railroad tracks was time-consuming and often dangerous work. Several inventors, including Thomas Edison, put themselves to the task of inventing a multiplex telegraph—one that would allow several telegraph operators to use the same line at the same time. (Remember, Alexander Bell and Elisha Gray were both attempting to invent the harmonic telegraph—a form of multiplex telegraph—when they turned their attention to the telephone instead.)

Multiplexing made telegraph service more efficient and cost-effective, but a larger obstacle still remained: Morse's code itself. Sending messages via Morse code required a trained operator at each end of the wire. Western Union and its competitors were keen to develop a system that did not require constant human intervention.

As early as 1846 (only two years after Morse's first successful telegraph demonstration), a man with the unlikely name of Royal House invented a printing telegraph. Unfortunately, House's machine had its own set of problems. Although House claimed his machine was "twice as fast as Morse," it required two operators at each end of the line.

Several other inventors worked on printing telegraph machines, but French inventor Emile Baudot made many of the breakthroughs. Baudot's printing telegraph was the first to use a typewriterlike keyboard, and it allowed eight machines to share a single wire. More importantly, Baudot's machines did not use Morse code. Baudot's five-level code sent five pulses down the wire for each character transmitted. The machines themselves did the encoding and decoding, eliminating the need for operators to become proficient at Morse code. For the first time, electronic messages could be sent by nearly anyone.

English inventor Donald Murray expanded and improved on Baudot's work, and Murray sold the American rights to his inventions to Western Union and Western Electric. The Murray patents became the basis for the teletypewriter, also known by AT&T's brand name Teletype and by its generic nickname, TTY.

Western Union applied the new technology on its own network. Over time, the teletypewriter replaced the Morse key and sounder in most of Western Union's offices. Western Union also used the teletypewriter technology to provide a service called telex. Telex service allows subscribers to exchange typed messages with one another. Until the advent of the fax machine in the 1980s, telex service was widely used in international business.

AT&T operated a similar service called the Teletypewriter Exchange (TWX). Like telex, TWX service consisted of a teletypewriter connected to a dedicated phone line. TWX had the advantage of access to AT&T's wide-reaching telephone network. Like telex, TWX usage peaked in the 1960s and 1970s. In 1972, AT&T sold the TWX service to its old nemesis, Western Union.

In the 1930s and 1940s, several schemes were developed to allow the transmission of Teletype signals via shortwave radio. Radio Teletype, or RTTY, uses a technique called frequency shift keying (FSK) to simulate the on and off voltage used by conventional teletypes. In FSK, a signal on one frequency indicates ON, and a signal on the other indicates OFF. Since radio signals can be keyed on and off very quickly, RTTY signals run at speeds similar to land-line teletypewriters.

RTTY signals broadcast via shortwave radio allow many stations to receive the same signal. RTTY was widely used by United Press International (UPI) and the Associated Press (AP) wire services before cheaper, more reliable satellite links became available in the 1980s. RTTY in various forms is still used today for ship-to-shore telex service and for marine and aeronautical weather information.

The Teletypewriter

For fifty years after its invention at the turn of the century, the teletypewriter was the mainstay of nonvoice electronic communications. Teletypewriters were frequently connected in a round-robin circuit. In this configuration, the original signal is sent from one point on the circuit and received by all the other machines on the circuit. This type of circuit was widely used by news wire services such as the Associated Press and United Press International.

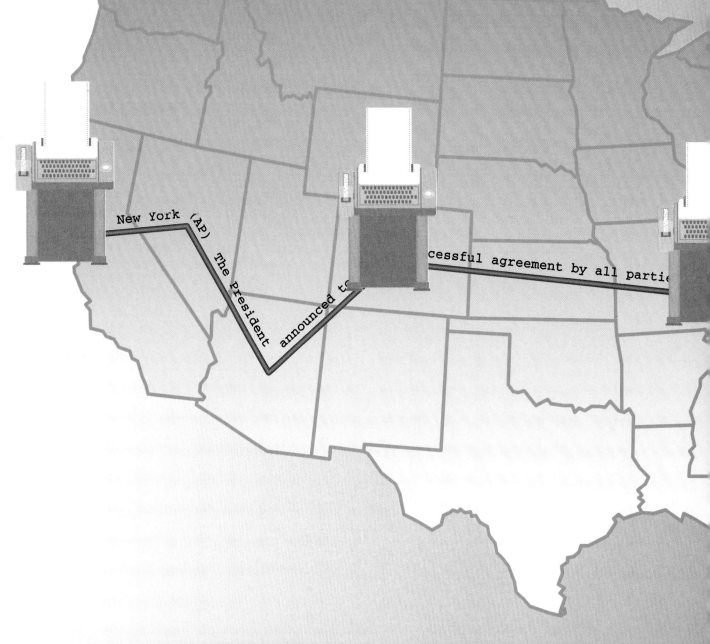

New York (AP) The President announced t... ...cessful agreement by all parti...

Unlike the Baudot code, Morse code uses characters of unequal length and size. For example, the letter E is expressed as one dot, but the number 0 is expressed as five dashes. This inequality of size makes Morse easy to detect by ear but very difficult to decode mechanically.

The Baudot code uses five equal-length elements (Morse would have called them "dots") to define each character of the alphabet. Five elements can define only 25, or 32, different combinations—not enough to print the entire alphabet plus numerals and punctuation marks. To overcome this problem, two special nonprinting characters, called Figs and Ltrs, shift the printing mechanism between letters (A–Z) mode and figures (numbers and punctuation marks) mode. The two modes allow the code to represent a total of 62 characters.

BAUDOT
CODE SIGNALS
red denotes positive current

art	1	2	3	4	5	stop		
							A	-
							B	?
							C	:
							D	$
							E	3
							F	!
							G	&
							H	#
							I	8
							J	bell
							K	(
							L	
							M	

Seven countries endors

and Business Act.

International Free Trade

P A R T

2

MIXING COMPUTERS AND TELEPHONES

ALTHOUGH

they are products of different eras and different technologies, the computer and the telephone seem to have been made for one another. Today's telephone network could not exist without vast computing resources to process calls, route traffic, and print telephone bills. Conversely, the existence of a worldwide telephone network allows computers to connect to one another so that the machines (and their users) may exchange information.

Even though the computer and the telephone have been forced into a marriage of convenience, they are worlds apart. The computer's universe is digital: Everything that passes through the computer's CPU is either a 1 or a 0. The worldwide telephone network is largely digital, too—except for the last few miles of wire between the customer's home or office and the telephone company's switching equipment. In order to maintain compatibility with the millions of existing telephones, the local loop from the telephone company central office to the phone jack on your wall is the same two-wire circuit used by the Bell system since the 1890s.

AT&T was one of the first companies to adopt computers on a very large scale, and AT&T, through its Bell Labs subsidiary, funded some of the earliest computer research. The invention of the transistor at Bell Labs in 1948 made large-scale computers practical. AT&T also invented the first practical telephone modem—a device that allows digital data to travel via the analog world of the telephone network.

CHAPTER

4

The Early Networks

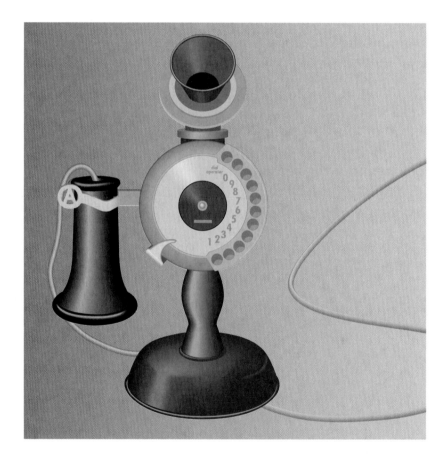

WHEN you hear the word *network* today, you probably think of computer networks, television networks, cable television networks, or local area networks. All of those networks owe their existence to two earlier networks: Western Union's network and the Bell system.

Western Union holds a special place in history: It was the world's first telecommunications giant. The completion of its first overland telegraph line ended the brief, exciting history—1860 to 1861—of the colorful pony express. Western Union was formed by the merger of 12 smaller companies. By the time of the Civil War, Western Union's lines stretched across the United States, from New York to California.

Western Union's network was the first to span the North American continent. Following the railroad westward, Western Union struck deals with most of the railroads of the day. In exchange for access to the railroad right-of-way, Western Union provided a telegraph station and an operator at each train station. The operator handled schedule and load information for the railroad at no charge.

Western Union's service was point-to-point. To send a telegram to someone, you would go to the Western Union office and dictate the message to the telegraph operator. The operator would then send the message out in Morse code over the telegraph line to the appropriate station.

When Bell Telephone began operations in the late 1890s, it had no telephone lines. As subscribers signed up for service, Bell ran new lines to the subscribers' locations. Initially, telephone service was also point-to-point, meaning that each phone could connect to only one other phone. Many of the early telephone subscribers were doctors; they would connect one phone in an office to another at home. As telephone service grew, subscribers wanted to be able to talk to one another—so the telephone network, as we know it today, was born.

Today's public telephone network is a complex maze of telephone lines and central switching offices. The central offices connect to an even more complicated web of cables, microwave towers, fiber optic cables, and communications satellites.

At one time, more than 90 percent of these facilities belonged to the Bell system. Since the court-ordered AT&T breakup in 1984, the facilities belong to dozens of companies, including AT&T, the regional Bell operating companies, MCI, GTE, and others. Despite all the behind-the-scenes complexity, the system remains easy to use. To make a call, you simply pick up the phone and dial the number.

The Telephone Network

1 The early telephone network was built by using iron or copper wire hung from wooden poles. Each telephone required its own two-wire pair to connect the telephone to the phone company's equipment. As the number of telephones exploded, so did the number of telephone wires. Today, many telephones are still connected to a central office using a two-wire connection that Alexander Bell would recognize.

2 All telephones are connected to a central office. In many cases, fiber optic cables, microwave radio, and satellite dishes have replaced the traditional copper wire. The central office connects calls between subscribers in the same central office and routes calls to other central offices or long-distance facilities.

3 Many calls, especially overseas calls, travel by satellite radio circuits. AT&T and Western Union pioneered the use of communications satellites.

4 An increasing number of calls travel by fiber optic cable. One hair-thin fiber optic cable can handle as many as 4,032 telephone conversations simultaneously.

5 ISDN is an all-digital telephone service that provides excellent quality voice and fast data communications over conventional twisted-pair copper phone lines. Each ISDN line provides two channels, and each channel can be used independently of the other for voice or data calls.

6 Many large offices use special, high-density phone lines. Digital T1 lines provide 24 communication channels that can be used for voice or data, and each channel can have its own phone number. Many phone companies offer "partial" T1 lines that provide the convenience and reliability of T1 for companies that don't need all 24 lines.

CHAPTER

5

From Keypunches to Terminals to the Carterfone

As we write this chapter, we're sitting in front of a 21-inch color screen with 1,024 by 768 pixel resolution in 256 colors. The keyboard has 103 keys, many of them reserved for special functions such as moving paragraphs or underlining a passage of text. As we type, our keystrokes instantly appear on the color screen, the text formatted and displayed exactly as it will appear when this page is printed. The printer can faithfully reproduce 35 different typefaces with 600 dot-per-inch accuracy.

But the earliest computers didn't have any of these features—in fact, they didn't even have a keyboard and screen. The very first computers used a variety of input and output devices, including switches, lights, teletypewriters, and paper-tape readers.

Because early computers were used primarily by scientists for one specific task, there was no pressing need to make data input and output faster or easier. But when computers became available and affordable for general business use, efficiency and accessibility became important concerns.

The first input/output device to find widespread acceptance was the keypunch and card reader combination. Data to be input to the computer was typed into a keypunch machine. The machine translated the operator's keystrokes into a series of holes punched in a card. The cards were then carried to the computer room, where they were placed into a card reader. The card reader "sensed" the holes in the cards and recreated the operator's keystrokes.

The punched-card system had many drawbacks: It was cumbersome, the cards could easily get out of order, and the input/output cycle took time—sometimes days or weeks. The punched-card system also had advantages: The keypunch machines could be located anywhere, and card decks from multiple locations could be sent to one central location for processing. Keypunch operators didn't require extensive training, since the keypunch keyboard resembled a standard typewriter keyboard. But the biggest disadvantage of the punched-card system was that it allowed only one program to run on the computer at one time.

The next step forward in the human-machine interface was the interactive printing terminal. Instead of punching holes in a card, the terminal sent keystrokes directly to the computer. The computer responded by sending characters to the terminal's printer. The early interactive terminals were usually teletypewriters or specially modified electric typewriters. With the advent of the time-sharing operating system, several operators could run jobs on the same computer at the same time. These machines were cantankerous and noisy, but they provided an immediate response from the computer—something the punched-card system could never do. The ability to get immediate answers from the computer led to a host of new applications for computer technology.

Perhaps the most significant of these new applications was the online processing system like those used in airline reservation systems. Using special leased telephone lines, airlines could place terminals in every city they served. Ticket agents across the country could use the central computer system to check fares and book flights. The online processing concept was and still is used in many other industries, including the computer industry itself.

Before the interactive terminal, programmers had to develop computer programs using punched cards. The delays and additional errors introduced by the punched-card system made an already difficult job even more difficult. The interactive terminal allowed programmers to see the results of their work immediately, thus reducing the amount of time required to develop a program.

Although the interactive printing terminal added a lot to the world of computing, it also left a great deal to be desired. Printing terminals are, by nature, mechanical devices. Even though they're faster than punched cards, they're still relatively slow, noisy, and require a great deal of maintenance.

In the mid-1960s, several manufacturers began to replace the terminal's printing mechanism with a picture tube, and the video display terminal (VDT) was born. VDTs work much like printing terminals do, but they are faster, quieter, and more efficient. The earliest microcomputer systems—the immediate predecessors to today's personal computers—also used VDTs for input and output.

In 1966, a small Texas company called Carterfone invented a simple device that allowed mobile two-way radios to connect to a telephone line. The Carterfone allowed construction workers, field service personnel, and traveling executives to make and receive telephone calls via their company's existing two-way radio system.

The Carterfone did not physically connect to the phone line. Nevertheless, AT&T maintained that the Carterfone posed a threat to the integrity of the telephone system. After a two-year battle, the FCC ruled that third-party equipment could indeed be connected to the telephone network as long as the connected device contained protective measures to ensure that no harm could come to the telephone network. The Carterfone decision was the beginning of the end of AT&T's near-monopoly on telephones and telephone-related equipment.

In 1975, the FCC went a step further. The FCC ruled that any piece of equipment could be attached to the telephone company's lines, if the device met certain technical specifications. In 1977, the FCC published these technical specifications, known as Rules and Regulations of the Federal Communications Commission, Part 68: Connection of Terminal Equipment to the Telephone Network. The rules, commonly known as Part 68, describe how third-party equipment should connect to the telephone network. If you look on the bottom of almost any telephone or modem sold in the United States today, you'll see a sticker stating that the device conforms to Part 68 of the FCC rules.

The FCC's Part 68 rules opened a floodgate of new equipment. Dozens of manufacturers jumped into the telephone business. Instead of paying a few dollars every month to the local phone company, you could buy a phone of your own. Telephones became available in every imaginable shape, size, and color. Telephone accessories such as answering machines, cordless phones, and modems became common household items. The telephone industry itself was turned upside down, all thanks to a little company from Texas.

Punched Card

The punched card was the primary means of data input and output for many years. The card itself was made of heavy paper and could store 80 characters of information—one in each column. The card and method of coding date back to a mechanical vote-counting machine invented by Herman Hollerith in 1890.

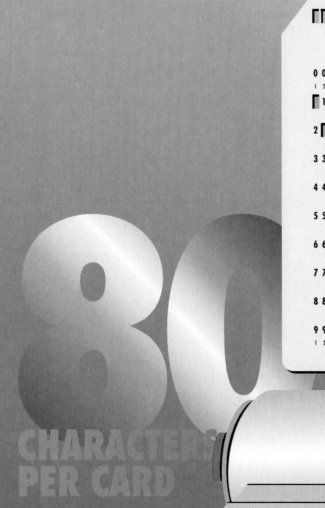

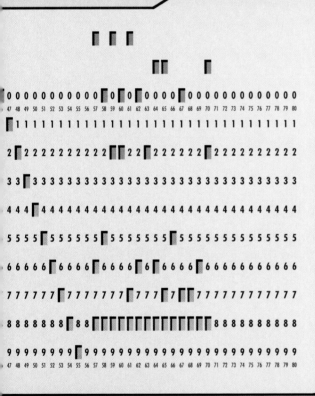

A typical 2 Gigabyte hard drive stores the equivalent of 25 million punched cards. An equivalent stack of punched cards would be 5 miles high!

Terminals and the Carterfone

IBM Selectric Terminal

The IBM Selectric printing terminal was the first interactive printing terminal designed specifically for use on a computer system. Earlier printing terminals were derived from teletypewriters, but the Selectric machine was a completely new design.

The Selectric introduced IBM's now-famous golf ball rotating-type element. Although the Selectric was more reliable and created more attractive type than its predecessors did, it wasn't any quieter.

Early Video Display Terminal

The Lear-Siegler ADM-3A terminal shown here wasn't the first video terminal, but it was one of the most popular. The ADM-3A could display 24 lines of 80 characters each.

Designed in the pre-microprocessor era, the ADM-3A contained a hard-wired logic board—essentially a dedicated narrow-purpose computer system in itself. The logic board's dual purpose was to store incoming data in the video memory of the terminal and to send keyboard keystrokes to the host computer.

Because so many computer operators were accustomed to teletypewriter keyboards, most early VDT keyboards followed teletypewriter conventions for placement of the punctuation and special characters. Early Apple computers also used this layout.

The Carterfone

It may not look like much, but this simple device turned AT&T's equipment business upside down. Because the Carterfone engineers weren't allowed to connect their equipment directly to the Bell system lines, they chose a method called acoustic coupling to pass sound between the two-way radio and the telephone line.

The top portion of the Carterfone was made of molded plastic. When a radio user needed a telephone connection, the radio operator at the base station placed a telephone handset into the Carterfone and dialed the call. Inside the Carterfone, an induction microphone picked up sound from the telephone receiver, and a miniature speaker talked into the telephone microphone.

CHAPTER
6

Alphabet Soup: Morse, Baudot, ASCII, and EBCDIC

LIKE Morse code before it, Emile Baudot's five-level teletypewriter code introduced the world to a faster, more efficient form of communications. Baudot's code, with improvements and additions made by English inventor Donald Murray, served as the primary code used in machine-to-machine communications for over fifty years. But despite its longevity, the Baudot code had several shortcomings.

As we saw in Chapter 3, the Baudot code uses 5 bits of data to represent each transmitted character. A special shift code is used to shift the receiving machine between letters and figures mode. Even with the shift code, the Baudot code can only accommodate uppercase letters.

In 1966, several American computer, teletypewriter, and communications companies collaborated to devise a replacement for the Baudot code. The result of their work is the American Standard Code for Information Interchange, or *ASCII*. ASCII uses a 7-bit code, allowing it to represent 128 discrete characters without using a shift code. ASCII defines 96 printable characters (the letters A through Z in upper- and lowercase, numbers 0 through 9, and punctuation marks) and also includes several control characters that define nonprinting functions such as carriage return, line feed, and backspace.

Besides offering full upper- and lowercase printing, ASCII also defines a simple error-checking mechanism. An extra bit, called the parity bit, is added to each transmitted character. If the communications circuit is using even parity, then the parity bit is set to 0 when there is an even number of bits in the transmitted character. If the circuit is using odd parity, the parity bit is set to 0 when there is an odd number of bits. Although parity checking doesn't provide a means to retransmit corrupted characters, it does provide a simple validity test for received data.

ASCII was widely and readily adopted by most computer and communications equipment vendors worldwide (IBM was the notable exception). Beyond the improvements ASCII offered over Baudot, ASCII provided a well-defined public standard that didn't owe its existence to any one company. As an added bonus, any ASCII-standard computer could, at least in theory, exchange information with any other ASCII system.

IBM, following a long-standing tradition of doing things its own way, did not adopt ASCII. Instead, IBM engineers devised their own code, called EBCDIC, for Extended Binary Coded Decimal Interchange Code. EBCDIC is an 8-bit code, so it can define a total of 256 different characters. This is its one advantage over ASCII. Unlike ASCII, the alphabetic characters in EBCDIC are not sequential, making sorting operations more difficult.

Although it is still widely used in IBM mainframes and minicomputers, EBCDIC never caught on in the non-IBM universe. IBM itself has shunned EBCDIC on several occasions, most notably in the design of the IBM Personal Computer and its successors.

From Morse Code to EBCDIC

Because Morse code was meant for human ears, it contains data elements of unequal length. The dash is three times the length of the dot, and a period equal to one dot is added between letters, so the receiving operator can discern one letter from the next.

The five data elements of Baudot code (called "bits" today) are of equal length to define each character. Because 5 bits allow only 32 combinations, Baudot code uses two special characters called FIGS and LTRS to tell the receiving machine to print the figures character set or the letters set. This effectively doubles the number of code combinations to 64. Baudot code is uppercase only, and the characters are not in sequential numerical order: For example, A has a value of 24, B is 19, and C is 14.

ASCII improves on Baudot code in several key ways. The use of 7 data elements, or bits, allows ASCII to represent up to 128 discrete characters: 31 characters are reserved for such special functions as carriage return, backspace, and line feed, and 96 characters are reserved for the letters A through Z in upper- and lowercase, as well as numbers and punctuation marks. ASCII characters are in sequential order: A is 65, B is 66, C is 67, and so on. This facilitates computer manipulation of ASCII text and numbers.

IBM's EBCDIC uses 8 data bits, allowing it to represent 256 discrete characters and symbols, of which 63 characters are reserved for control functions. In this table, A is 193, B is 194, C is 195. However, EBCDIC is not sequential: Its character set—unlike ASCII's—does not follow sequential order. There are gaps between i and j and again between r and s.

A

MORSE

BAUDOT

16 8 4 2 1

$16 + 8 = 24$

ASCII

64 32 16 8 4 2 1

$64 + 1 = 65$

EBCDIC

128 64 32 16 8 4 2 1

$128 + 64 + 1 = 193$

⬤ = ON BITS   ⚪ = OFF BITS

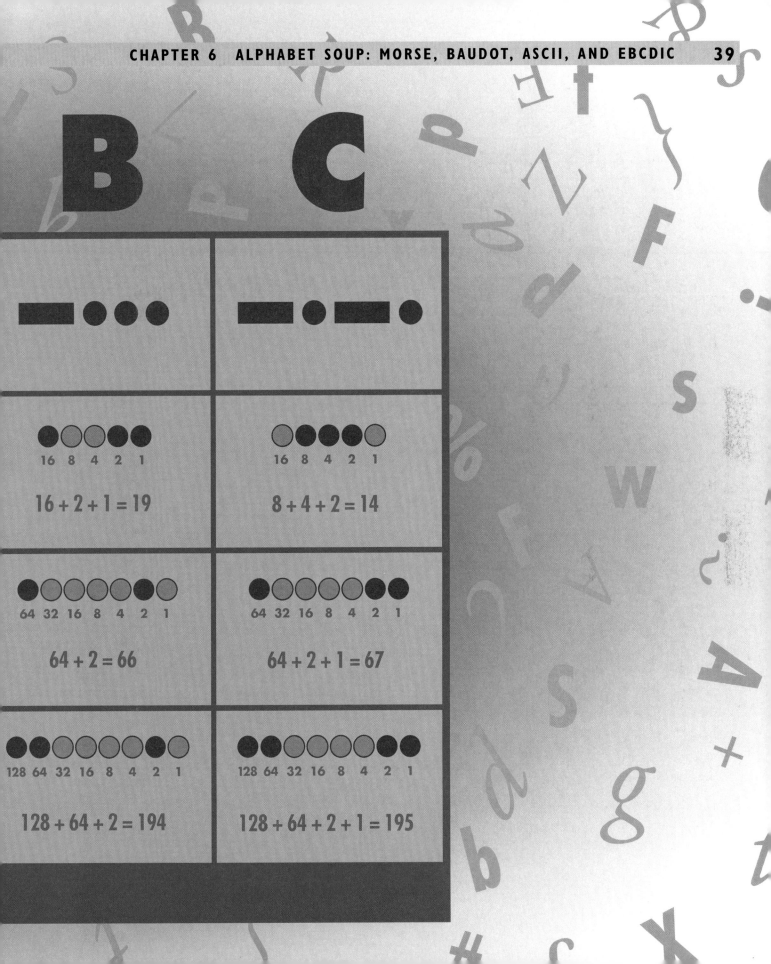

CHAPTER

7

The Bell 103 Modem

THE early electronic communications devices—the telegraph and teletypewriter—communicated with one another by exchanging pulsed direct current (DC) signals over a long wire. Modern-day computers and terminals use an improved version of this technique, as defined by the RS-232C and other computer communications standards.

Telephones, in contrast, communicate by passing an analog audio signal over the line. The strength and frequency of the signal varies depending on the volume and pitch of the sound being sent. Because the telephone network is designed to carry voice signals, it cannot carry the DC signals used in computer communications.

As the use of computers spread in the late 1950s and early 1960s, a need arose to connect computers and terminals via ordinary telephone lines. AT&T's answer was the Bell 103 modem. A modem (that is, a *mod*ulator/*dem*odulator) converts the on-and-off digital pulses of computer data into on-and-off analog tones that can be transmitted over a normal telephone circuit.

The Bell 103 modem operated at a speed of 300 bits per second. This is painfully slow by modern-day standards, but it was fast enough for the slow-printing terminals of the day. Because it allowed the terminal to be physically separated from the host computer, the modem made computing resources available from virtually anyplace.

Recent improvements in modem technology allow speeds up to 57,600 bits per second, 192 times the speed of the original Bell 103 modem. As we'll see in Chapter 11, these modems use microprocessors to achieve these high communications speeds. Ironically, some newer modems contain more computing power than many early mainframe computer systems!

Regardless of the communications speed, all modems share some common characteristics. Since they must connect to a computer or terminal, virtually all modems contain an RS-232C communications interface. Similarly, most modems also contain an RJ-11 telephone-line interface—the familiar clear plastic four-wire telephone plug.

The Bell 103 modem uses two pairs of tones to represent the on-and-off states of the RS-232C data line. One pair of tones is used by the modem originating the call, and the other pair is used by the modem answering the call. The modem sends data by switching between the two tones in each pair. The calling modem sends data by switching between 1,070 and 1,270 hertz, and the answering modem sends data by switching between 2,025 and 2,225 hertz.

Newer modems use more and different tones to convey information, but the basic principle remains the same.

A Modem Connection

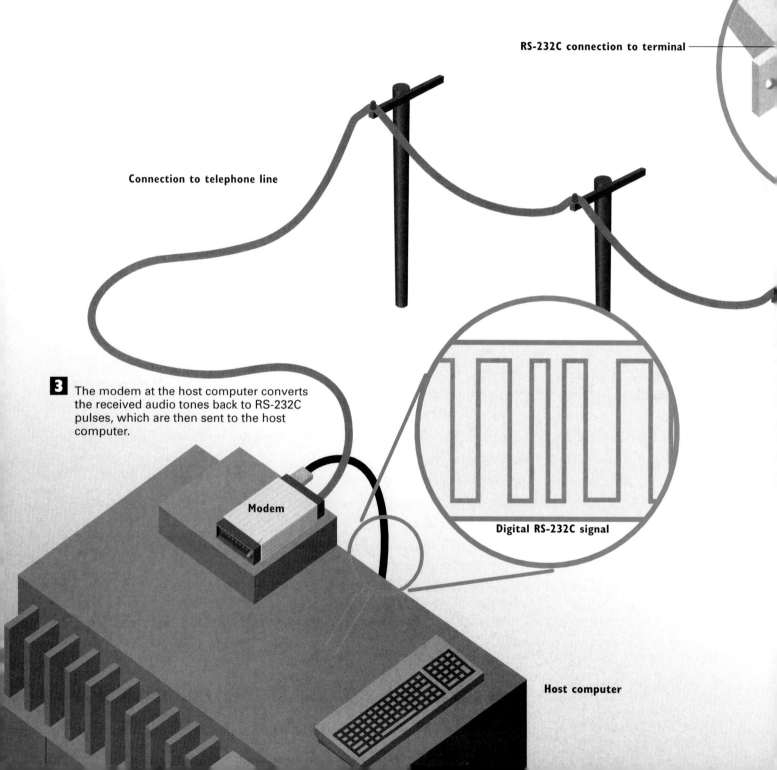

RS-232C connection to terminal

Connection to telephone line

3 The modem at the host computer converts the received audio tones back to RS-232C pulses, which are then sent to the host computer.

Modem

Digital RS-232C signal

Host computer

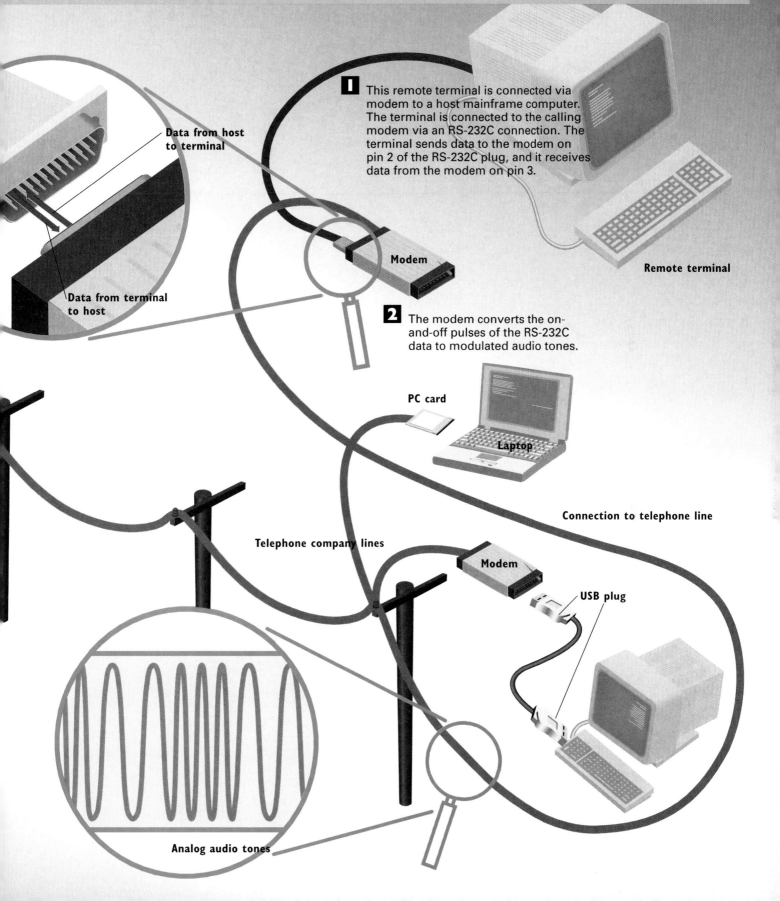

Data from host to terminal

Data from terminal to host

1 This remote terminal is connected via modem to a host mainframe computer. The terminal is connected to the calling modem via an RS-232C connection. The terminal sends data to the modem on pin 2 of the RS-232C plug, and it receives data from the modem on pin 3.

Modem

Remote terminal

2 The modem converts the on-and-off pulses of the RS-232C data to modulated audio tones.

PC card

Laptop

Connection to telephone line

Telephone company lines

Modem

USB plug

Analog audio tones

CHAPTER
8 Dialing for Data

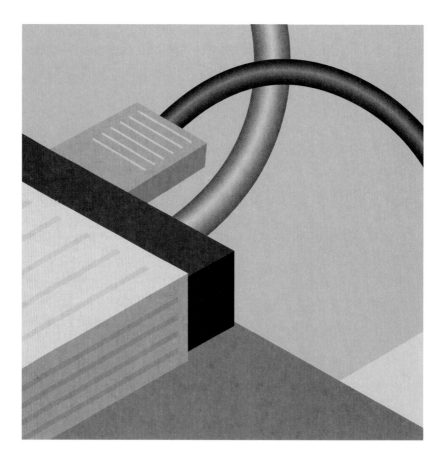

EARLY computer systems were very large and very expensive. A typical mainframe computer cost millions of dollars and required several hundred square feet of specially air-conditioned office space. In addition to the hardware, early computers required a full-time staff of programmers and technicians to keep them running. Despite the enormous costs involved, thousands of businesses and universities installed mainframe computer systems in the 1960s and 1970s. Many of those systems are still in use today.

One of the major developments of the 1960s in computing technology was the concept of time-sharing. A time-sharing system allows more than one user—often as many as several hundred—to use the same computer simultaneously. Users could run their own programs, and each user interacted with the computer via a terminal. Most of these early mainframe terminals were mechanical teletypewriter-type units. By the mid-1970s, the video display terminal (VDT) had replaced printing terminals for many applications. Because VDTs often replaced aging teletypewriters, they became known as "glass Teletypes."

In most multiterminal systems, the terminals connected directly to the host computer via a cable. IBM, in typical IBM style, devised its own proprietary system to connect terminals to host computers. However, other manufacturers, including Digital Equipment Corporation, Data General, and Honeywell, used RS-232C connections between the host and the terminals. And for users located away from the main computer site, terminals equipped with modems could be used to access the host computer.

These connections then allowed terminals to move out of the computer room and onto users' desktops. This seemingly simple relocation had a huge effect on the way people used computers. By allowing hundreds of users to share the same computer system, the cost per user spiraled downward. Suddenly, it made economic sense to use computers for such mundane tasks as accounting, classroom scheduling, and even word processing. Before time-sharing, computing was the domain of very large corporations and research institutions. By reducing the cost per user, mainframe computers became affordable for many smaller companies and colleges.

The development of the microprocessor and the accompanying personal computer explosion of the late 1970s began a trend away from terminals and towards desktop computing. In effect, the computing power moved out of the mainframe computer room and onto the users' desktops. As PCs became cheaper and more powerful, it appeared that mainframe computers and the whole idea of a central processing unit were dead. But in the late 1980s, a new type of time sharing arrived on the scene. A new breed of shared computers called *application servers* allows several users to offload specialized tasks onto a shared computer. In effect, these systems do exactly what the time-sharing systems did—they rely on one centralized processor to perform a specific task.

Host Computer and Terminals

A typical large computer system consists of a host computer system—a mainframe or a minicomputer—and a network of terminals. The terminals, located in the same building as the host, usually connect directly to the host system.

If large branch offices have more than one terminal, a device called a statistical multiplexer can be used to combine the RS-232C signals from the terminals into one multiplexed signal. Another multiplexer at the host computer site reconstructs the individual RS-232C signals from each terminal.

Medium-sized offices requiring full-time access to the host system can be equipped with special leased telephone lines. Although these lines are expensive to install, they are usually cheaper to operate and more reliable than long-distance dial-up lines.

Two banks of modems—one for regular dial-up telephone lines and one for special leased lines— allow off-site access to the host computer.

Small offices needing occasional access to the host computer use a regular voice-grade telephone line and a dial-up modem to access the host system.

CHAPTER

9

The RS-232C Serial Interface

THE earliest electronic communications devices—the telegraph and teletypewriter—communicated by switching on and off voltage on a wire. The voltage used varied according to the equipment in use and the length of the wire involved. The circuit between two machines typically allowed communication in one direction at a time.

Today's high-speed data communications equipment still operates on the principle of switching voltage on and off, but many improvements have been made to the basic communications circuit. In an attempt to ensure that one serial device will talk to another, the Electronics Industries Association (EIA) created a standard to define the electrical signaling and cable connection characteristics of a serial port. In 1969, the EIA established Recommended Standard (RS) number 232 in version C, or RS-232C, the most common type of communications circuit in use today.

The ASCII character set defines what numbers to use for each character, and the RS-232C standard defines a way to move the data over a communications link. Commonly used with ASCII characters, RS-232C may also be used to transmit Baudot or EBCDIC data.

The RS-232C standard defines the function of the signals in the serial interface as well as the physical connection used by the interface. This standard defines two classes of serial connections: one for terminals, or *DTE* (Data Terminal Equipment), and one for communications equipment, or *DCE* (Data Communications Equipment). A DTE device usually connects to a DCE device. For example, a personal computer (DTE) can connect to a modem (DCE). The serial port on most personal computers is configured as a DTE port.

An RS-232C connection normally uses a 25-pin D-shell connector with a male plug on the DTE end and a female plug on the DCE end. Rules (and EIA standards) were made to be broken, and many manufacturers have taken liberties with the hardware they use to implement the RS-232C standard. When the IBM PC/AT first appeared in 1984, IBM decided to use a 9-pin connector for the serial port. The AT's serial port shares an expansion card with a parallel printer port. There isn't enough room on the card bracket for two 25-pin plugs, so IBM abbreviated the serial connector to a 9-pin plug. Other manufacturers followed suit, so you may encounter either type of connector on your desktop computer, and you'll certainly find 9-pin connectors on laptop and notebook computers. Some manufacturers provide both 9-pin and 25-pin connectors for the same serial port.

The RS-232C Serial Interface

An RS-232C serial connection consists of several independent circuits sharing the same cable and connector. There are two data circuits (send and receive), and there are several control circuits, called handshaking lines, which control the flow of data between the terminal and the host.

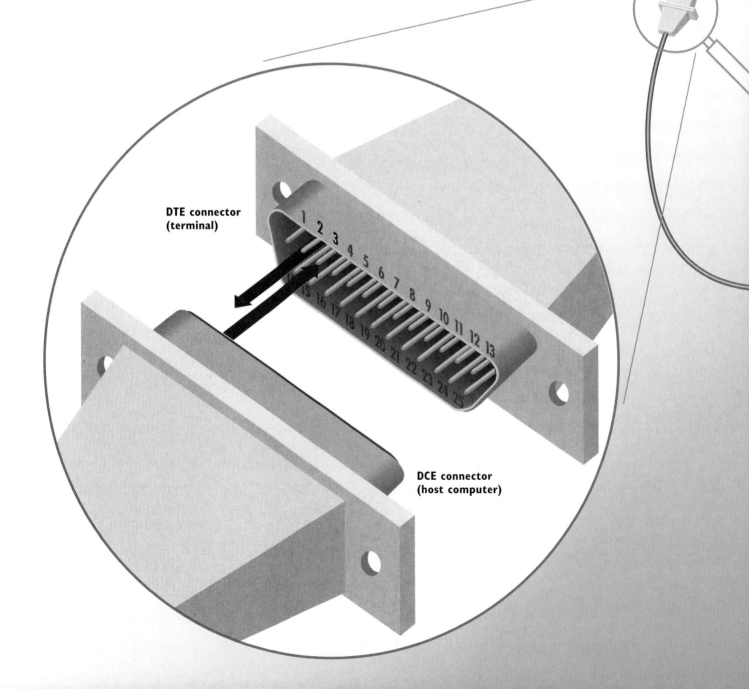

DTE connector
(terminal)

DCE connector
(host computer)

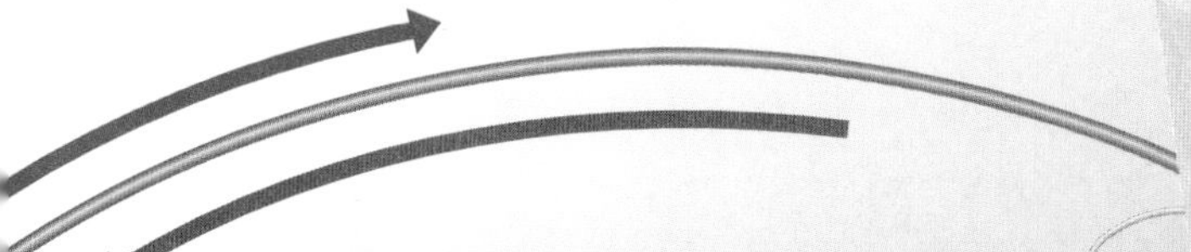

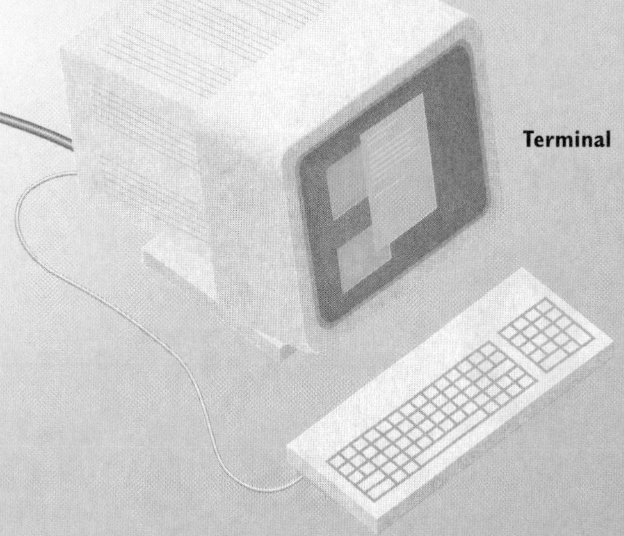

Terminal

The most important part of the RS-232C interface is the data path. There are two circuits in the data path: one from the DTE (Data Terminal Equipment) to the DCE (Data Communications Equipment), and another from the DCE back to the DTE. In this example, the terminal sends data to the host computer on pin 2 of the cable and receives data from the host on pin 3. Pin 7 serves as the ground connection for both circuits.

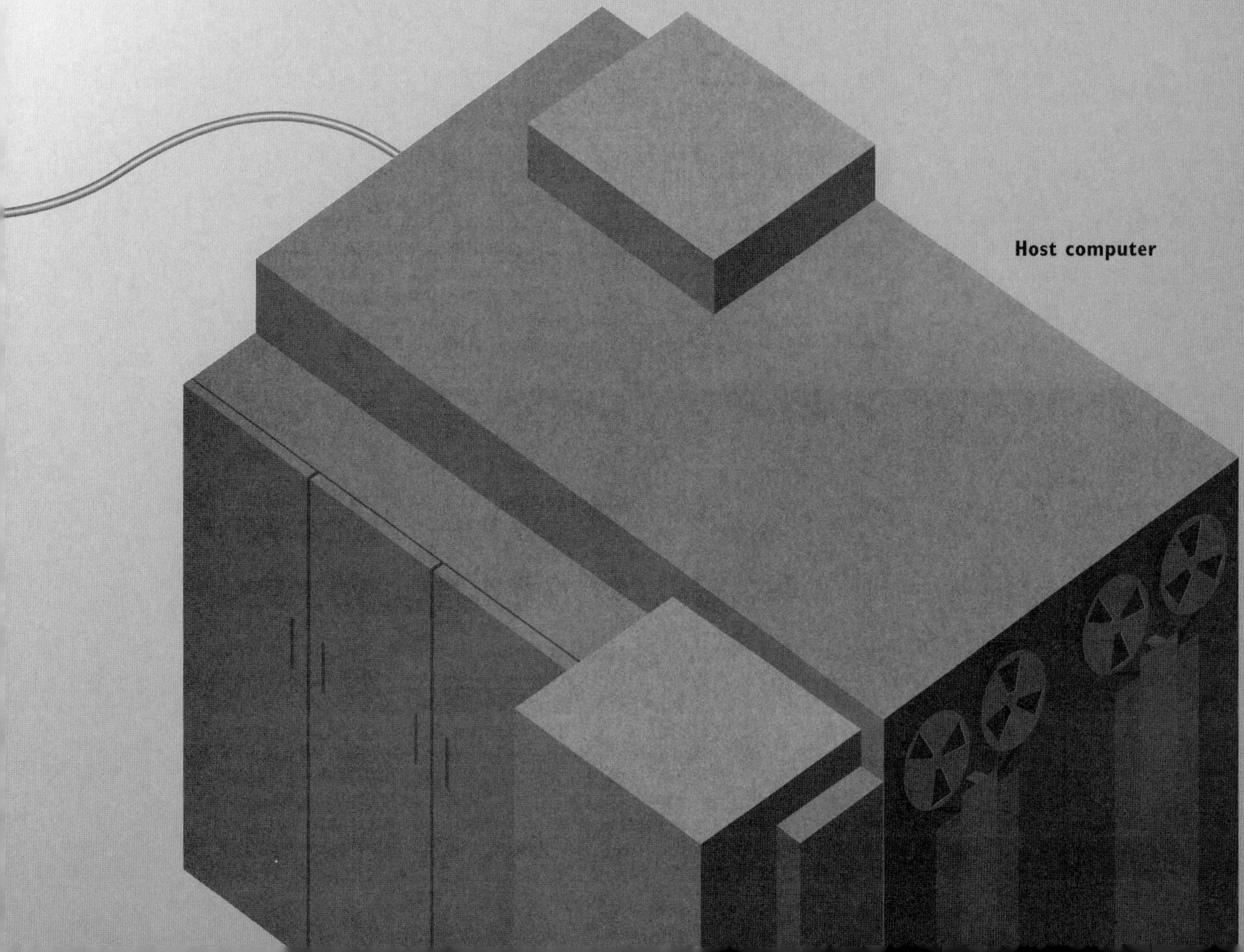

Host computer

CHAPTER

10

The Personal Computer as a Terminal

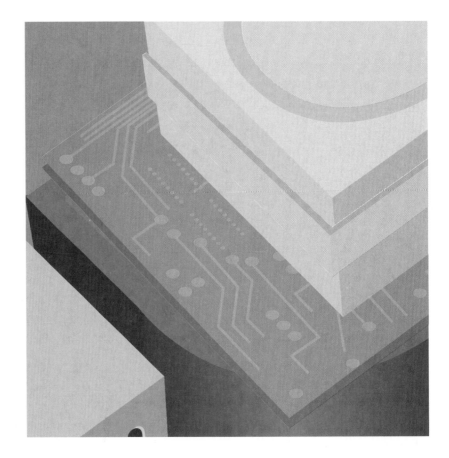

MAINFRAME

and minicomputer systems may have dozens or even hundreds of terminals attached to them. This allows many users to share the mainframe's CPU, disk storage, and other resources. A typical terminal looks much like a personal computer; it contains a video display, a keyboard, and a serial interface. Unlike a personal computer, a terminal can't do anything unless it is connected to a host computer. When connected, the terminal displays incoming data on the video screen and sends keyboard input to the host computer. Communication with the host computer takes place through the serial interface. The central computer does all the work, and the remote terminals provide a way for users to communicate with the central computer. This type of system is called a Shared Processor system.

Personal computers first appeared on the computing scene in the late 1970s. In many cases, those early personal computers were purchased by medium and large companies, most of which already had a larger computer system. At first, these computers were used as stand-alone systems; thousands of them were purchased just to run one application such as Lotus 1-2-3, VisiCalc, or WordPerfect.

It wasn't unusual to see an office with a personal computer on one corner of a desk and a mainframe terminal at the other. Before long, these same companies learned that by adding a communications program to the personal computer, they could use the computer as a terminal and save all that precious desktop space.

Personal computers are routinely used as the access point to the company's mainframe or minicomputer system. Rather than placing both a personal computer and a terminal on everyone's desk, many companies have retired their terminals and replaced them with computers. With the proper communications software, a personal computer can perform all the functions of a terminal. In most cases, a personal computer with communications software actually offers more features than the terminal it replaces.

Over the past few years, the cost of processing power has plummeted. Today's desktop PCs have as much or more processing power as the mainframe and minicomputer systems of ten years ago. As a result, many companies have retired their mainframe and minicomputer systems and replaced them with a network of personal computers. Instead of sharing one large, powerful, and expensive processor on the mainframe, networked systems—also called distributed computing systems—spread the computing workload among the PCs on the network. Each PC operates independently of the others, yet any PC can share files, printers, and other resources with the other computers on the network. We'll take a more detailed look at networked computing in Part 3.

Distributed processing systems have many advantages, the most important being that they're often cheaper than a central processor system. They're also more reliable in many ways because no one component is essential to the system's operation. But distributed systems have their own problems. Because they share the work among dozens or hundreds of PCs, distributed systems require a great deal more maintenance than a central processor system. Networked PCs are often difficult to maintain; each new operating system and application software release must be installed on each and every PC on the network. PCs are also susceptible to computer viruses and user configuration problems, resulting in costly service calls.

In a back-to-the-future effort to blend the best of the distributed and centralized computing worlds, two new computing models have evolved. The network computer and thin client computing models are variations on a similar theme. Instead of putting a complete computer on every user's desk, network computers provide users with a bare-bones computer with no hard disk, floppy drive, or CD-ROM drive. Network computers must load all of their applications over a LAN from a network server. Thin clients are similar to network computers, but many thin client machines have some form of local storage—typically a floppy drive—for saving work in progress.

As you can see, network computing is a hybrid of distributed and centralized computing models. By storing all of the programs and data on a central server, network administrators regain control over their organization's computing resources. Because users can't install programs on their own machines, they can only run authorized software—this greatly reduces the risk of computer viruses.

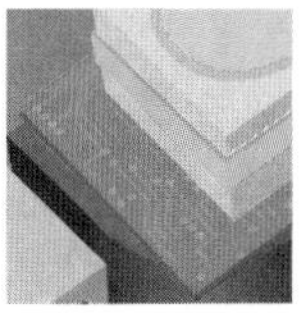

The Personal Computer as a Terminal

1 Users communicate with mainframe and minicomputer systems via terminals. Each host computer may have dozens or hundreds of terminals attached to it. Terminals have a keyboard and a display screen. The screen is typically a text-only display, although specialized graphical terminals are also available. Terminals have no storage or intelligence; all programs run on the mainframe system, and all data is stored on the mainframe's disk system.

2 In recent years, many organizations have replaced their mainframe and minicomputer systems with a network of PCs. PCs have their own processor, graphical display, and disk storage, and each PC's program runs independently of the others on the network. Special, high-performance PCs called File Servers allow individual client PCs to use the shared disk, printers, and other resources connected to the server. While this arrangement provides excellent performance and flexibility, it does so at a high cost, in terms of equipment, software, and ongoing maintenance.

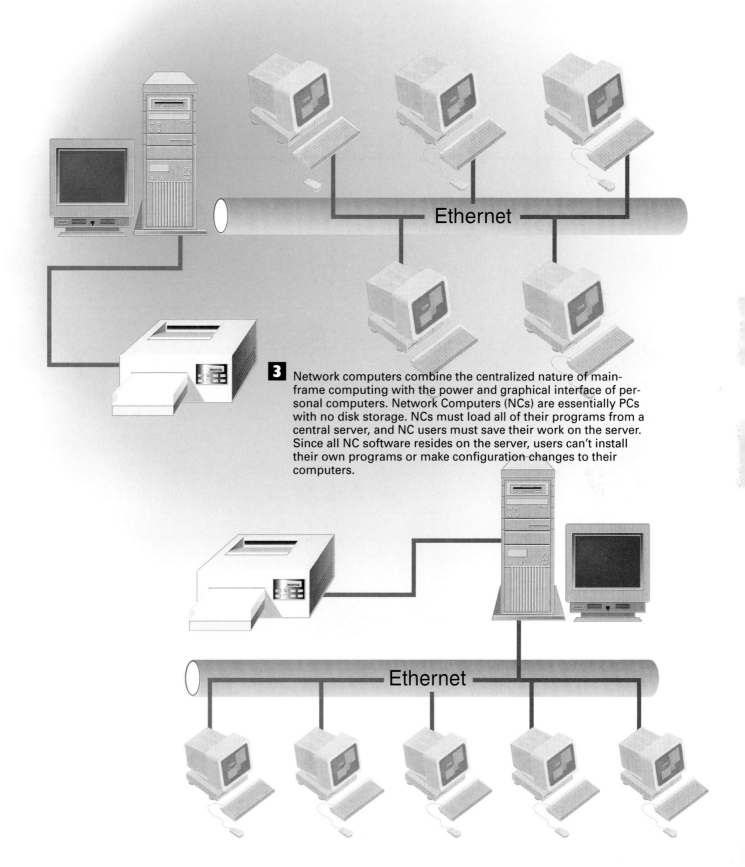

3 Network computers combine the centralized nature of mainframe computing with the power and graphical interface of personal computers. Network Computers (NCs) are essentially PCs with no disk storage. NCs must load all of their programs from a central server, and NC users must save their work on the server. Since all NC software resides on the server, users can't install their own programs or make configuration changes to their computers.

Ethernet

Ethernet

CHAPTER

11

Smart Modems

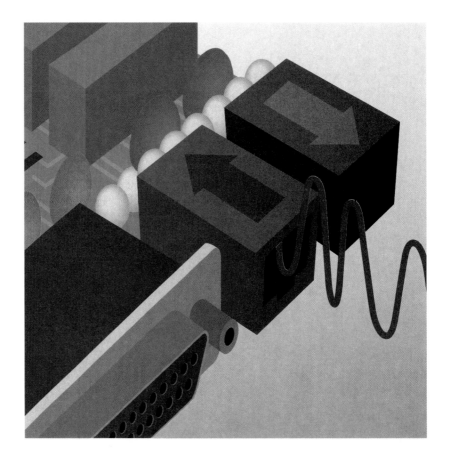

As we saw earlier in this book, modems connect the digital universe of computers to the analog world of the telephone network. The earliest modems designed by Bell Labs operated at a maximum speed of 300 bits per second. Almost as soon as the first modems went into service, users began clamoring for faster, more reliable modems. The clamor continues today, even though modern-day modems operate at speeds up to 56,000 bits per second.

The next step up from the 300bps Bell 103 modem was another AT&T product, the Bell 212a modem. This modem operated at 1,200 bits per second, or four times the speed of the earlier 103 unit. Although the higher operating speed was a big improvement, the 212a units were very susceptible to noise and signal degradation on the telephone circuit.

Before the Bell system breakup in 1984, AT&T set virtually all modem standards. Bell Labs' engineers designed new modems, and AT&T's Western Electric division manufactured them. Bell licensed the 103 and 212a technology to other companies, but, with few exceptions, all new modem designs came from AT&T. After the breakup, AT&T was no longer in a position to dictate standards to the rest of the industry.

The Bell breakup coincided with the boom years in personal computer growth. By 1984, the personal computer industry was in the midst of a period of phenomenal growth, which began with the introduction of the IBM Personal Computer in late 1981. The personal computer explosion, coupled with the Bell breakup, presented some unique business opportunities for America's modem manufacturers.

One company in particular, Hayes Microcomputer Products, took the lead in the personal computer modem business. Hayes pioneered the use of microprocessor chips inside the modem itself. Unlike other modems, the Hayes unit could take the phone line off the hook, wait for a dial tone, and dial a telephone number all by itself.

Like most innovations in the computer industry, the Hayes modem was quickly and mercilessly copied by other modem makers. But Hayes was there first, and it holds one of the key patents relating to intelligent modems.

The next major advance in modem technology was the development of the 2,400 bits-per-second modem in 1985. Until 1985, most modem technical standards had come from AT&T's Bell Labs. The 2,400bps standard was created by the CCITT—an industry standards-setting organization comprising members from hundreds of telecommunications companies worldwide. The new modem standard—designated V.22bis—was widely accepted and is still in use today.

The CCITT—now called the International Telecommunication Union-Telecommunication sector (ITU-T)—continues to mediate industry standards for modems. Newer ITU-T standards include V.32 (9,600bps), V.32bis (14,400bps), V.34 (33,600bps), V.42 (error control), V.42bis (data compression), and V.90 (56,000bps). Virtually all modems in use today conform to one or more ITU-T standards, assuring compatibility between modems worldwide.

Today's 56,000bps V.90 modems represent what is likely to be the end of the road for analog modem development. The laws of physics and the need to maintain compatibility with the existing telephone network represent an insurmountable roadblock to faster analog modems. Fortunately, several other communication technologies offer fast, reliable connections.

Inside a Modem

Here's a peek under the hood of a typical 33.6/56Kbps modem. The modem has four major areas: power supply, subscriber interface, CPU, and modem circuitry.

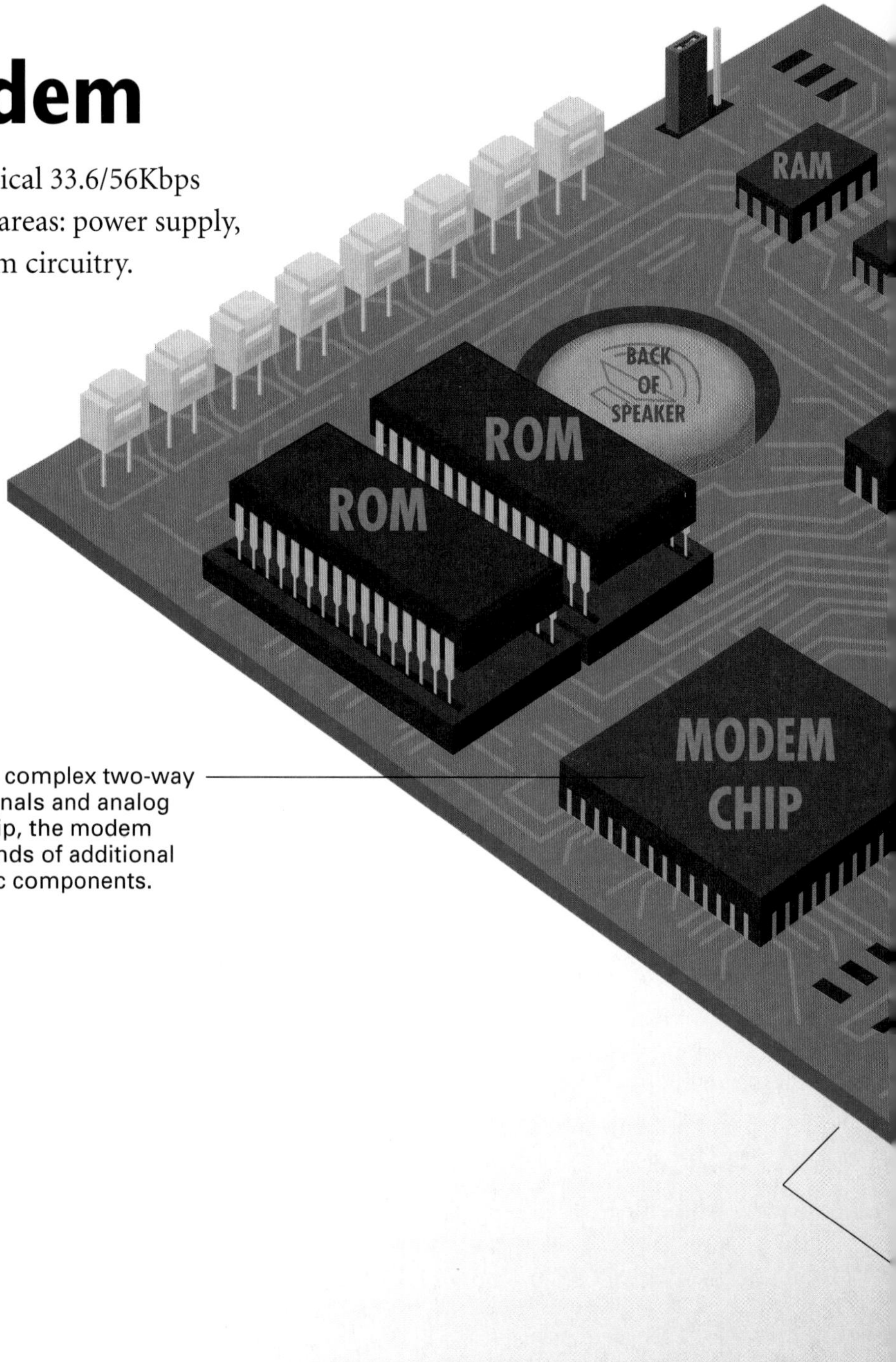

RAM

BACK OF SPEAKER

ROM

ROM

MODEM CHIP

The modem chip performs the complex two-way conversion between digital signals and analog sound signals. Without this chip, the modem circuitry would require thousands of additional transistors and other electronic components.

Like any computer, the modem's CPU circuitry requires a steady, regulated source of power. The on-board power-supply circuitry converts the AC power provided by the power transformer into regulated DC power.

The central processing unit, or CPU, is the heart of the modem. The CPU controls virtually every other component of the modem and performs the data compression and error detection specified by the CCITT protocols. The CPU's program loads from ROM chips and uses RAM for temporary storage. Flash ROM makes it possible to upgrade modems to conform to new standards.

The analog side of the modem begins with the subscriber-line interface, which connects to the telephone network. Overload circuitry protects the modem from lightning and other electrical hazards. Additional circuitry ensures that the modem's output signal conforms to the FCC Part 68 rules.

CPU

RS-232C

The RS-232C interface connects the modem to a terminal or host computer. Directed by commands received through the RS-232C port, intelligent modems can store and dial telephone numbers automatically.

ISDN

Integrated Services Digital Network (ISDN) is an all-digital telephone service that provides reliable voice and data communications using the same wiring as the existing telephone network. ISDN provides two 64Kbps connections that can be combined into one 128,000bps connection. Each of the two 64Kbps channels operates independently of the other, and each channel can be used for voice or data communication. Phones attached to ISDN lines can place and receive calls to conventional analog phones, and most ISDN lines have two phone numbers, one for each of the two channels. After several years of false starts, ISDN is now widely available in most of North America. Pricing varies widely, but in many places a single ISDN line is cheaper than two POTS lines.

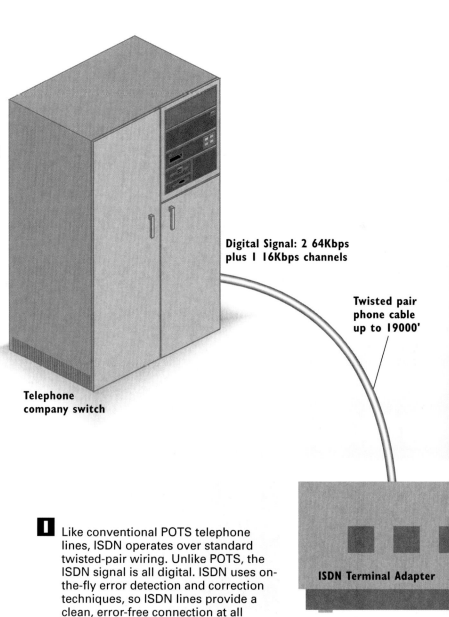

Digital Signal: 2 64Kbps plus 1 16Kbps channels

Twisted pair phone cable up to 19000'

Telephone company switch

ISDN Terminal Adapter

1 Like conventional POTS telephone lines, ISDN operates over standard twisted-pair wiring. Unlike POTS, the ISDN signal is all digital. ISDN uses on-the-fly error detection and correction techniques, so ISDN lines provide a clean, error-free connection at all times.

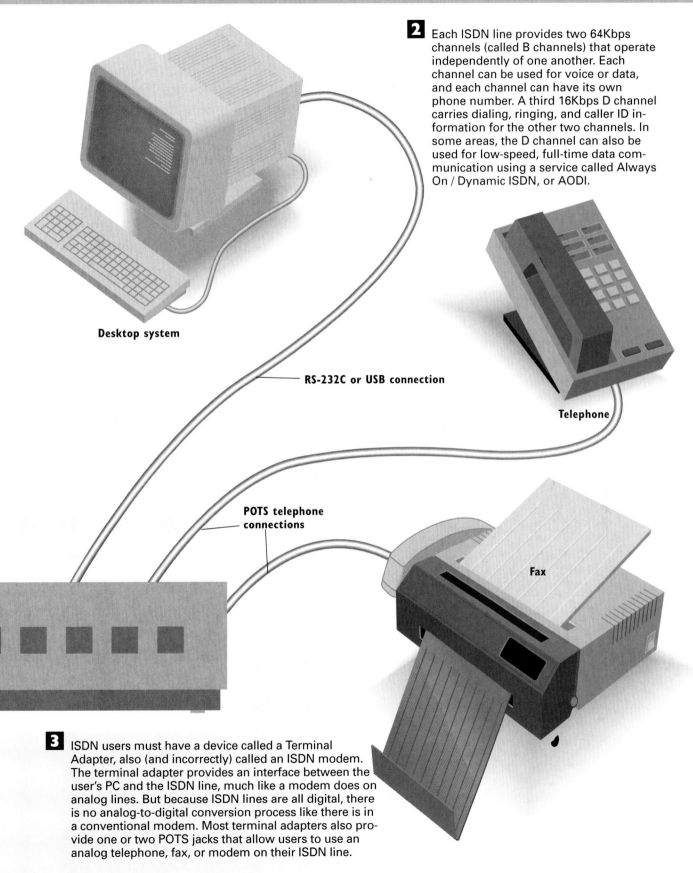

2 Each ISDN line provides two 64Kbps channels (called B channels) that operate independently of one another. Each channel can be used for voice or data, and each channel can have its own phone number. A third 16Kbps D channel carries dialing, ringing, and caller ID information for the other two channels. In some areas, the D channel can also be used for low-speed, full-time data communication using a service called Always On / Dynamic ISDN, or AODI.

Desktop system

RS-232C or USB connection

Telephone

POTS telephone connections

Fax

3 ISDN users must have a device called a Terminal Adapter, also (and incorrectly) called an ISDN modem. The terminal adapter provides an interface between the user's PC and the ISDN line, much like a modem does on analog lines. But because ISDN lines are all digital, there is no analog-to-digital conversion process like there is in a conventional modem. Most terminal adapters also provide one or two POTS jacks that allow users to use an analog telephone, fax, or modem on their ISDN line.

DSL

Digital Subscriber Line (DSL) is another new technology that is just now becoming available in limited test markets. Like ISDN, DSL uses existing telephone network wiring to deliver an all-digital connection. DSL service can share a wire path with a conventional phone line, so you can receive DSL service and conventional phone service on the same wire. Unlike ISDN, DSL provides a single data channel, and that data channel is a dedicated point-to-point circuit, usually used to connect a home or office directly to an Internet Service Provider. There are several incompatible varieties of DSL, but the key DSL providers and equipment vendors are working on a common standard. DSL speeds range from 384Kbps up to several megabits per second.

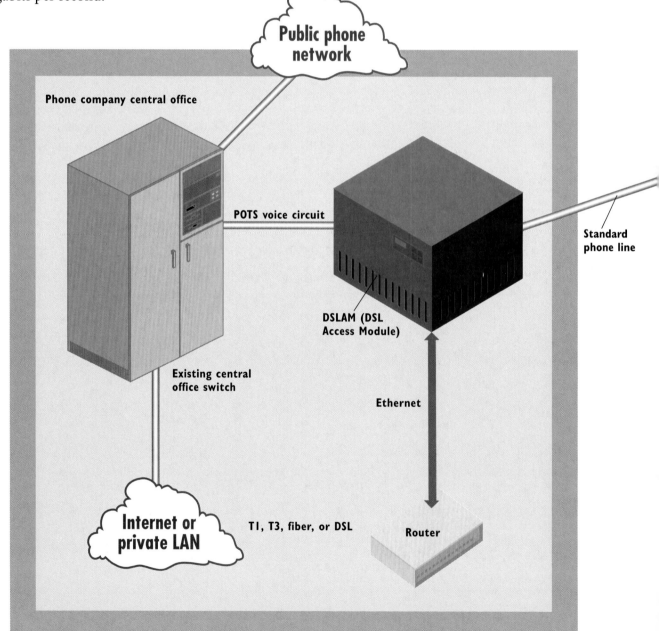

Public phone network

Phone company central office

POTS voice circuit

Standard phone line

DSLAM (DSL Access Module)

Existing central office switch

Ethernet

Internet or private LAN

T1, T3, fiber, or DSL

Router

1 There are several variants of DSL technology, but they all use ordinary, pre-existing copper telephone lines to deliver high-speed data service to users. DSL service can operate over the same pair of wires as an existing POTS phone connection. At the customer's end, a splitter box separates the DSL and POTS phone signals. Telephones, fax machines, and other devices attach to the POTS phone line as usual. The DSL splitter connects to a DSL modem, which in turn connects to the user's PC via an Ethernet connection.

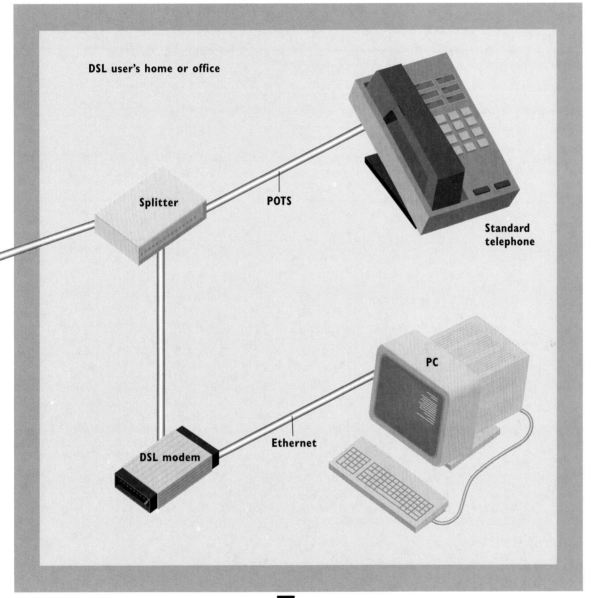

DSL user's home or office

Splitter

POTS

Standard telephone

PC

DSL modem

Ethernet

2 At the phone company's central office, a device called a DSL Access Module (DSLAM) separates the phone signal and connects it to the normal switched telephone network. The DSLAM also acts as a router. Typically, the router connects to an Internet backbone connection to provide Internet access for DSL users. In some areas, the phone company can route one DSL user directly to another. This allows the DSL connection to be used for remote LAN access.

Cable Modems

Cable modems deliver multi-megabit speeds by using your local cable company's cable TV network. Once thought to be an entertainment technology, cable modems have emerged as one of the frontrunners in the fast connection marketplace. Cable modems use one or two TV channels to transmit and receive data over the neighborhood cable. Although they aren't yet available in every market, many major cable operators see cable modems as the future of their industry.

User #3: TV, no modem

Television

2 All of the houses in a neighborhood share a common coaxial cable. The cable carries the usual cable TV signal, and it also carries a special signal that provides a two-way path for cable modems. Because cable modems are very fast—up to 10Mbps—they connect to your PC via an Ethernet connection, instead of the RS-232C serial port used by conventional modems.

Cable company premises

1 There are two basic types of cable modems; one-way and two-way. Both use the existing cable TV infrastructure to deliver an Internet connection to their customers. Although they use the same cable, cable modem and cable TV services are typically sold separately. You don't need to subscribe to cable TV to use a cable modem, and vice versa. This diagram shows how a two-way system works.

High speed link to Internet

3 Cable modems use one or two TV channels to transmit and receive data over the neighborhood cable. Several neighborhood cables connect to a concentrator, which combines the data from several neighborhood cables into one high-speed fiber-optic cable. The fiber-optic cable connects the concentrator to the main cable company facility, called the headend.

Hybrid fiber/coax

Hub

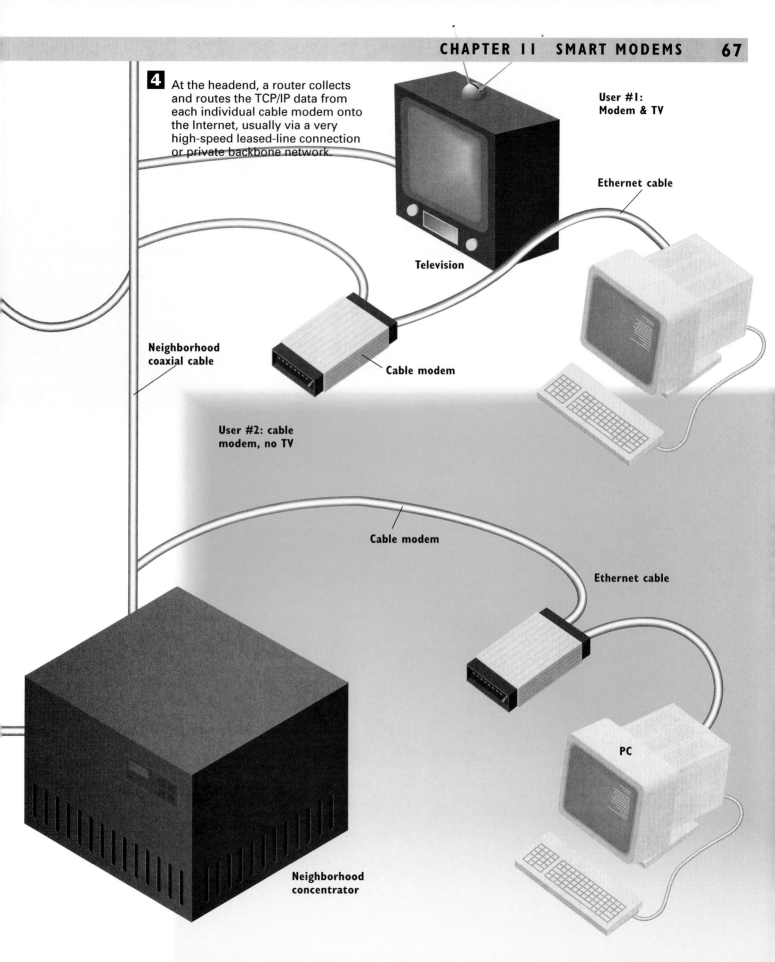

4 At the headend, a router collects and routes the TCP/IP data from each individual cable modem onto the Internet, usually via a very high-speed leased-line connection or private backbone network.

User #1: Modem & TV

Ethernet cable

Television

Neighborhood coaxial cable

Cable modem

User #2: cable modem, no TV

Cable modem

Ethernet cable

PC

Neighborhood concentrator

CHAPTER

12

Computer Telephony Integration

TELEPHONY

—first, you have to pronounce it right: *te-LEFF-in-nee*. Computer telephony integration (CTI) is the linking of telephones and computers to gain productivity. Affordable PC-based CTI can make your small business appear as a multinational corporation to callers. CTI running on mainframe computers has been a tool of multinational corporations for more than a decade.

A corporate *call center* is the term used to describe the workplaces of reservation clerks, order takers, and 911 operators—people who work hard to please the hard-to-please. The calls coming into these centers are often handled by a CTI device that performs a function called *call routing*. You know this as "Press 1 for new accounts, press 2 for information," and so on. But today, call routing can also be based on the telephone number of the originating caller. A service called *caller ID*, provided by the telephone company, identifies the calling number to the called party. In CTI call center systems, the clerk sees a screen identifying the caller and detailing any current account information before saying "Hello." Today, PC-based systems do an excellent job of call routing and of linking application programs to the incoming caller ID.

In *outbound call centers*, automated systems dial numbers until someone answers, then they buzz an idle clerk and make the phone connection. Do you get phone calls soliciting credit card and newspaper subscriptions during dinner? That's outbound calling CTI.

Many small businesses use PC-based CTI to set up private *voice mailboxes* for their employees. A PC equipped with a voice synthesis card and the appropriate software answers incoming calls and gives callers the choice of leaving a voice message for any of the employees. Often the system includes a search capability that allows callers to find employees and their mailboxes by last name. Employees can call into the same system, enter a few numbers from the telephone keypad, and retrieve messages. Telephone companies provide the same types of service to subscribers, but PC-based systems cost less in the long run.

There are many types of CTI products. Today, CTI functions such as voice mail are often included as a part of modems equipped with digital signal processing (DSP) chips. These chips are capable of voice synthesis and other telephone functions.

Incoming Call Routing

Caller dials a number

Telephone company central office

Telephone company completes the call and sends the ID of the caller to the destination.

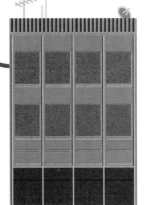

Based on the identity of the caller, the application program either directs the call to a recorded message or calls out records from a database and displays them for a clerk while ringing the clerk's phone.

An internal adapter decodes the caller ID and passes it to an application program.

Caller records and account history

Computer Telephony Integration

In tightly integrated CTI systems, a telephony server exchanges information and commands with the corporate private branch exchange (PBX) telephone system. PC-based applications can initiate calls, route calls, conference, and perform other functions through the PBX.

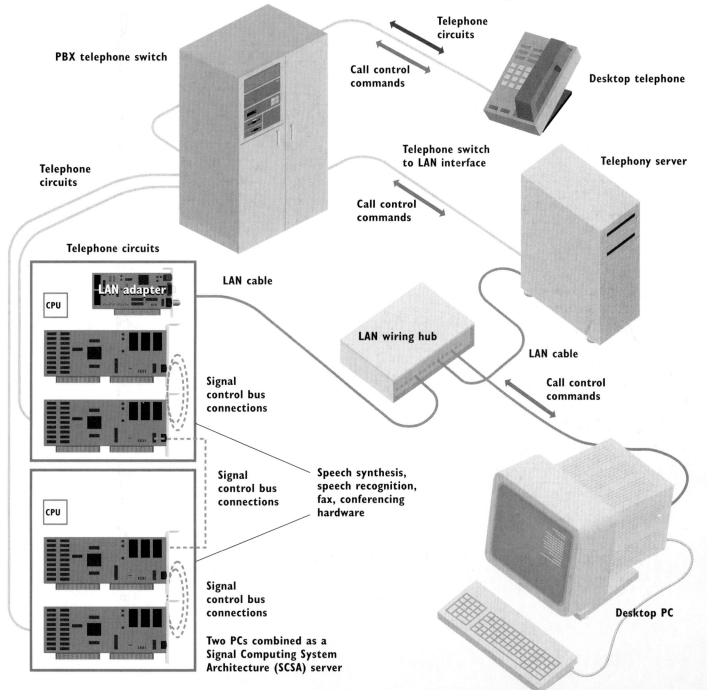

PBX telephone switch

Telephone circuits

Call control commands

Desktop telephone

Telephone switch to LAN interface

Telephony server

Telephone circuits

Call control commands

Telephone circuits

LAN adapter

CPU

LAN cable

LAN wiring hub

LAN cable

Call control commands

Signal control bus connections

Signal control bus connections

Speech synthesis, speech recognition, fax, conferencing hardware

CPU

Signal control bus connections

Two PCs combined as a Signal Computing System Architecture (SCSA) server

Desktop PC

How Multiplexed Voice, Fax, and Data Works

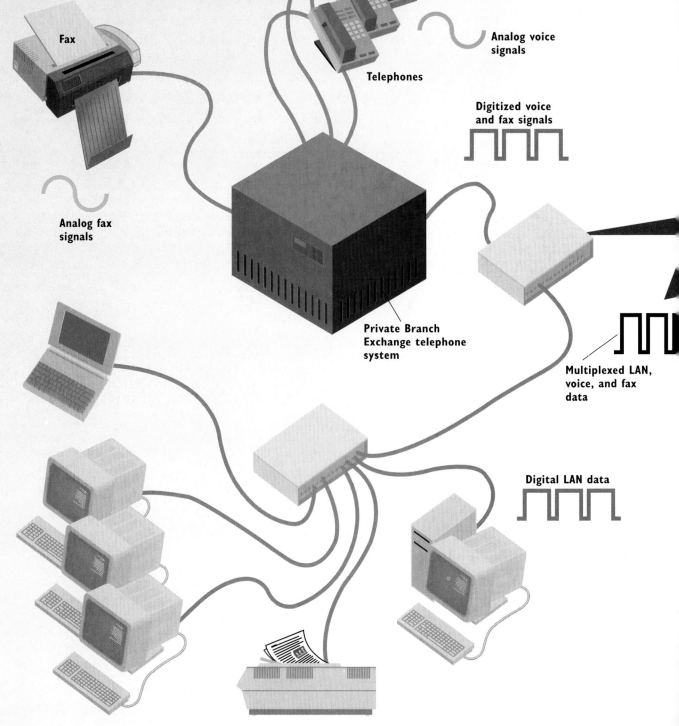

Fax

Telephones

Analog voice signals

Digitized voice and fax signals

Analog fax signals

Private Branch Exchange telephone system

Multiplexed LAN, voice, and fax data

Digital LAN data

"Bits is bits!" You probably won't find that explanation in an engineering textbook, but the point is valid. Once you convert any sound, image, signal, or event to bits, you can apply standard processing techniques to delay, transmit, or replay it. The commonality of bits becomes particularly useful when you want to fill up a communications channel to gain the best economy.

Computer data comes in bursts. Voice and fax data has a different rhythm. It is beneficial to mix the two in order to make the best use of the connections.

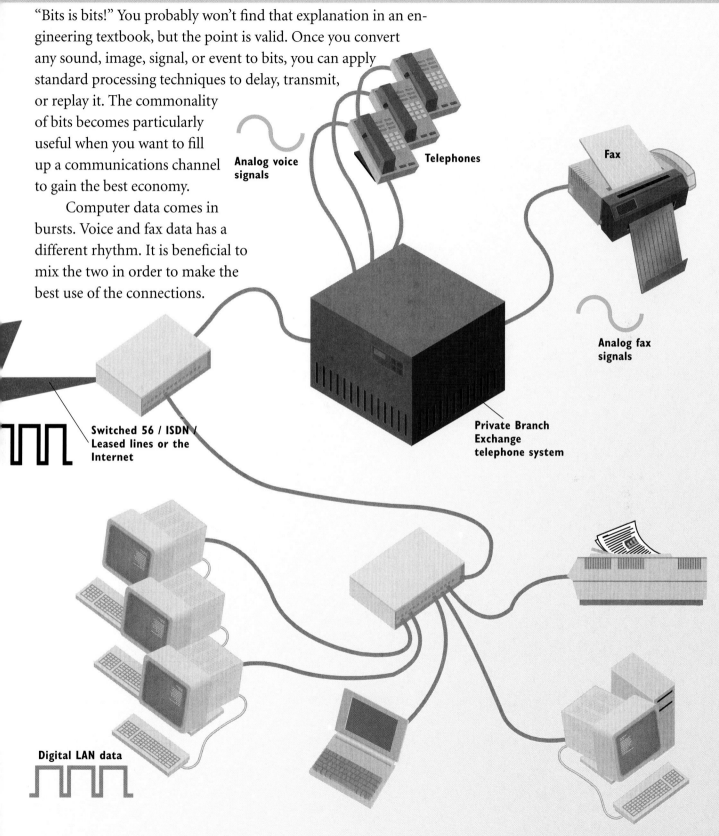

Analog voice signals

Telephones

Fax

Analog fax signals

Switched 56 / ISDN / Leased lines or the Internet

Private Branch Exchange telephone system

Digital LAN data

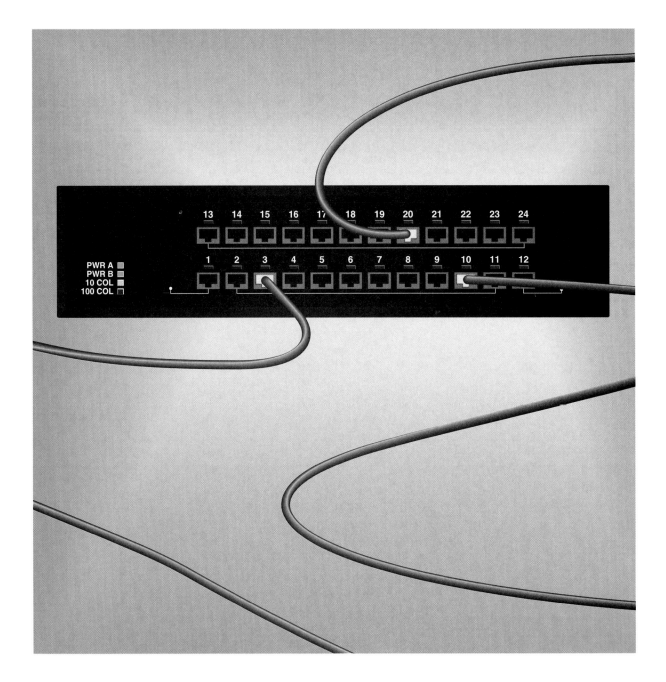

P A R T

LOCAL AREA NETWORKS (LANS)

UNTIL now, we've focused on how computers communicate—how they transmit and receive data. We looked at how they communicate with each other outside of an office when the distance between them makes it practical to use a modem or a fax instead of a disk or a piece of paper. In this part of the book, we're going to focus on how computers interoperate—how they work together in a network to improve your ability to get things done.

Networks are for sharing. Sharing such things as word processing and spreadsheet files, printers, communication links to distant computers and networks, and electronic mail systems is the function of a network. Every sharing activity, from car pools to bank lines, has its own rules. In networking, we call these rules standards and protocols. *Standards* describe how things should be; typically they set a minimum performance level. *Protocols* are sets of rules and agreements; they describe how elements interact. The key to understanding networking is understanding the standards and protocols that make it possible to interoperate without losing or abusing the shared files and devices.

In this section, we'll talk about standards, protocols, and sharing. First, let's spend a little time learning how many of these standards and protocols came about, then we'll talk more about sharing. Although the standards and protocols for computer communications go back to the work of Morse and Bell at the beginning of this century, the standards and protocols for computer interoperation did not emerge until the early 1980s. Three streams fed the computer networking flood: IBM, the U.S. Department of Defense (DOD), and the Xerox Corporation's Palo Alto Research Center. Later, other industry and professional organizations, particularly the Institute of Electrical and Electronic Engineers (the IEEE, pronounced *i-triple-e*) played an important part in developing standards, but the story starts with a computer system called SAGE.

The Semi-Automatic Ground Environment (SAGE) was developed by IBM for the DOD in the 1960s. SAGE, an air-defense system that operated until the mid-1980s, used vacuum-tube computers with memory banks so large that two people could stand inside of them. The computers were installed in pairs in blockhouse buildings, and the filaments from the tubes in a pair of SAGE computers supplied all of the winter heat for large three-story buildings in places such as Great Falls, Montana, and Duluth, Minnesota. The SAGE program involved the efforts of all the best U.S. communications and computer scientists in the 1960s and resulted in a network of interoperating computers that stretched across the United States. The program was the equivalent of the Golden Spike that linked the railroads in 1869. SAGE proved the practicality of interoperating computer systems and stimulated development efforts, particularly by IBM and the federal government.

In the 1970s, the DOD—faced with an inventory of different computers that could not interoperate—pioneered the development of network software protocols that work on more than one make and model of computer. The major set of protocols established by the DOD is the Transmission Control Protocol /Internet Protocol (TCP/IP). As the name implies, these protocols are agreements on how transmission takes place across networks. Companies, particularly those that want the federal government's business, write software that conforms to those protocols.

At about the same time in the 1970s, IBM began making public the standards and protocols it used for its proprietary computer systems. The standards included detailed descriptions of cabling, and the protocols were designed to ensure accurate communications under heavy loads. This work led others to emulate IBM's techniques and raised the quality of network development in the entire industry. It also led to an uprising by other computer companies that objected to IBM's total control of the most widely used standards and protocols. Eventually, this uprising led to the flexibility and interoperability we enjoy today.

Computer interoperation involves moving a lot of data, but it's difficult to move a lot of anything, including data, over a long distance. So computer interoperation usually begins with computers in the same office or the same building connected to a local network. The term *local area network*, or *LAN* (rhymes with *pan*), describes a group of computers typically connected by no more than 1,000 feet of cable, which interoperate and allow people to share resources.

In the 1970s, IBM and Digital Equipment Corporation developed ways for a few large computers to interoperate over local networks, but the most important work on LANs for a large number of computers was done at the Xerox Corporation's Palo Alto Research Center (PARC) in the late 1970s and early 1980s. At PARC, an important set of standards and protocols called Ethernet was conceived and developed to the point of becoming a commercial product. At about the same time, people working independently at Datapoint Corporation developed a standard called ARCnet, but Datapoint kept ARCnet as a proprietary set of specifications, so it didn't have the commercial success of Ethernet. Later, IBM developed the third major networking technology we use today, Token-Ring.

The early local area network architectures, such as Ethernet and ARCnet, combined inflexible hardware specifications with strict protocol descriptions. Specific types of copper cable, specific cable connectors, one physical configuration, and certain software functions were bundled together in each LAN definition. But because of the government and industry push for flexibility, the single simple set of specifications and descriptions for each type of network has expanded to include different types of cables, configurations, and protocols. Today, you can mix and match hardware and software to create a customized network and still stay within a network system specification supported by products from many different companies.

During the mid-1980s, a group of manufacturers started a movement toward what are called open protocols—protocols that do not favor a single manufacturer. Many manufacturers worked at developing software written to open protocol standards, but in the early 1990s, the movement lost momentum. The emphasis changed from developing a single set of new, openly published protocols to making practical use of the tried-and-true protocols of different manufacturers. As programmers and developers learned more about protocols and developed more programs and tools, they found ways to make different computers and networks interoperate without moving to a single rigid, but open standard. Today, it is easy to mix Macintosh and IBM-style personal computers on the same network and to interoperate among computers attached to different types of networks.

At the same time, new families of programs make it easier to share files and resources, such as printers and modems. In the 1980s, developers created the word processing, spreadsheet, and database programs that people use to create data files. In the 1990s, developers introduced new categories of software, referred to as workgroup productivity programs and workflow software, which make it easy to search for, organize, and link data from documents, spreadsheets, and databases so that it can be shared. Sharing now means more than just waiting in a queue to use a file or a printer. We have gone beyond the old computer model of data handling—which was like checking out one book at a time from the library to do research—and moved to new workgroup productivity programs that are the equivalent of having the librarian find the desired paragraph or reference, read it aloud to you, make a copy, and file it with other copies on the same subject. The availability of processed information transmitted over networks makes it possible for people to work faster and to work with fewer resources. This allows more people to work independently, to work at home, and to keep flexible hours.

Over a short few decades, the computer network industry has made more progress across a broad front than even the personal computer industry. The network evolution has swept along with it telephone technology, computer hardware design, software design, and even workgroup sociology. Today, both computers and buildings come with their networking components in place. If you have new equipment and a new building, you can add the software of your choice, plug a cable into a wall jack, and interoperate across a LAN. Wireless networks, both high-speed local networks and slower worldwide networks, link portable computers with a central business location. Modern networks mix handwritten and typed words, voice and sound, and graphics and video conferencing on the same cable. Networks make it possible for organizations to abandon the top-down management structure—that is, where a lot of information was held at the top—and move on to a flatter, more responsive structure where information is shared and widely available. Networks change the way we work, so now let's find out how they work!

CHAPTER

13

A Network Model

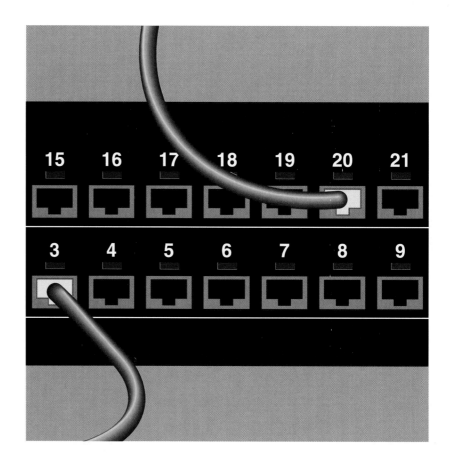

LET'**S** begin our investigation of networks by looking at their components to see how they relate to one another and connect. Then, in subsequent chapters we'll look inside each network component to see how it works. Here are the major components of a network:

Network Operating System   The network operating system, or NOS (rhymes with *boss*), consists of a family of programs that run in the networked computers. Some programs provide the ability to share files, printers, and other devices across the network. Computers that share their resources are called servers. Other programs that give the ability to use those shared resources are called clients. It is common to have client and server software running in the same computer, so you can use the resources on other computers while your coworkers make use of your disk space, printers, or communications devices.

Networked Peripherals   In 1991, a new category of products called networked peripherals became generally available; these include printers and modems with their own network connections. Network peripherals have internal specialized processors to run networking server software, so they don't have to be directly attached to a computer. Application programs running on client Macintosh computers and PCs can use a networked printer or modem as if it were locally attached.

Network Interface Card (LAN Adapter)   The low-powered digital signals inside a computer aren't powerful enough to travel long distances, so a device called a network interface card changes the signals inside a computer into more powerful signals that can cross a network cable. After the network interface card takes the data from the computer, it has the important jobs of packaging the data for transmission and acting as a gatekeeper to control access to the shared network cable.

Network Cabling   The computers in modern networks can send messages in the form of electrical pulses over copper cable of different kinds, over fiber optic cable using pulses of light, or through the air using radio or light waves. In fact, you can combine all these techniques in one network to meet specific needs or to take advantage of what is already installed. Modern network cabling installations use a wiring hub to isolate cable problems and improve reliability.

A Network Model

Networked Devices Devices such as printers and modems can have their own network attachments. The networking software makes it possible to use these shared devices as if they were locally attached.

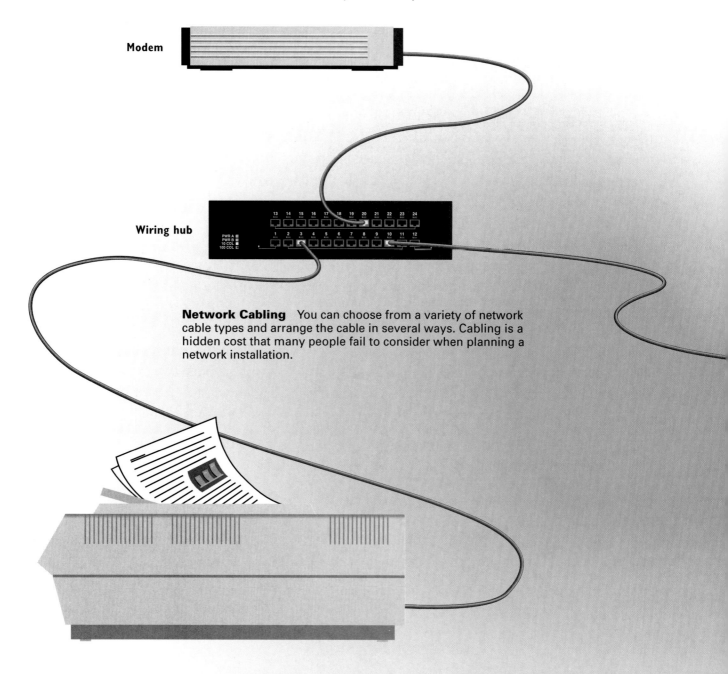

Modem

Wiring hub

Network Cabling You can choose from a variety of network cable types and arrange the cable in several ways. Cabling is a hidden cost that many people fail to consider when planning a network installation.

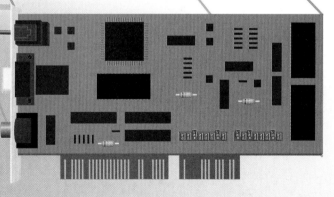

Networking Software   Networking software can be a separate product you add to your system, such as Novell's NetWare. Modern operating systems like Windows 95 and 98 and Windows NT include built-in networking functions. Apple's Macintosh computers come with networking software that allows them to operate on both NetWare- and Windows NT–based net-

Network Interface Card   Network interface cards link the computer to the network cable system. The card controls the flow of data between the computer's internal data bus and the serial stream of data on the network cable. Some computers come with their own network interface cards on the motherboard, and some interface adapters attach to a computer's parallel port, but the cards are usually added to the computer's expansion bus.

CHAPTER

14

Network Operating Systems

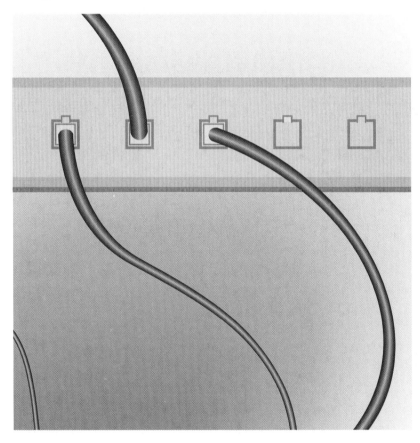

NETWORK operating systems, offered by companies such as Microsoft and Novell, are actually a combination of programs that give some computers and peripherals the ability to accept requests for service across the network and give other computers the ability to correctly use those services. Servers are computers that share their hard-disk drives, attached peripherals such as printers and CD-ROM drives, and communications circuits. Servers inspect requests for proper authorization, check for conflicts, and then provide the requested service.

File servers store files created by application programs. In some configurations, the file servers might also hold the application programs themselves. A file server is a computer that has a hard disk drive large enough to share. File servers provide the ability to simultaneously access the same file. People who update databases—customer-service representatives taking phone orders, for example—need to use the same inventory and financial data files at the same time. File-server software allows shared access to specific segments of the data files under controlled conditions.

Print servers accept print jobs sent by anyone across the network. Since even the fastest print jobs typically still take 5 to 10 seconds per page, *spooling* the print jobs (saving them in a disk file until the printer is ready to accept them) is a critical function of the print-server software. The print-server software also reports the status of jobs waiting for printing and recognizes the priorities assigned to specific users. Computers can run both the file-server and print-server software, or print-server software can run in specialized processors inside networked printers or in small self-contained print-server devices.

Client software works with the internal operating system of a computer so it can route requests from application programs and from the keyboard out to file servers and print servers on the network. The principal element of the client software is called a *redirector*. As its name implies, the redirector captures service requests it has been programmed to recognize and routes them out of the PC and across the network for service. Typically, redirector software is a built-in part of the client computer's operating system.

Network communications protocols package the requests from the client computers and send the requests across the network. Protocols handle the nitty-gritty details of addressing, routing, ensuring delivery, and ensuring accuracy. Typical suites of network communications protocols include Apple's Apple File Protocol (AFP), Microsoft's NetBIOS Extended User Interface (NetBEUI), and Novell's Sequential Packet Exchange and Internetwork Packet Exchange (SPX and IPX). Because the Internet is based on the TCP/IP protocol, many companies have adopted TCP/IP as their standard corporate networking protocol. TCP/IP is very flexible, and it can transport data on behalf of other protocols like NetBIOS.

You'll often hear people discuss the problem of having the proper drivers. The driver software works between the network interface card and the network communications software. If an adapter manufacturer supplies drivers conforming to Microsoft's Network Driver Interface Standard (NDIS) or Novell's Open Data-Link Interface (ODI), you can use that adapter with a variety of network operating systems.

Network Operating System Requests

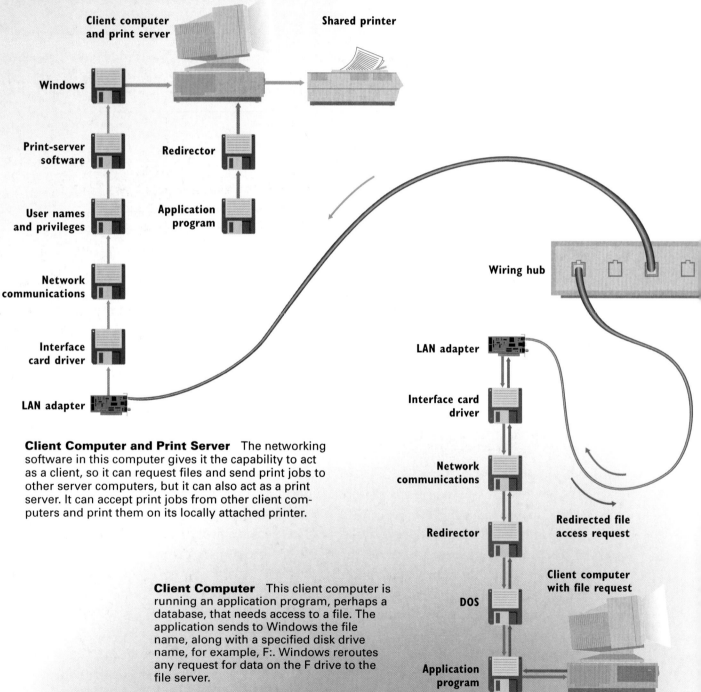

Client Computer and Print Server   The networking software in this computer gives it the capability to act as a client, so it can request files and send print jobs to other server computers, but it can also act as a print server. It can accept print jobs from other client computers and print them on its locally attached printer.

Client Computer   This client computer is running an application program, perhaps a database, that needs access to a file. The application sends to Windows the file name, along with a specified disk drive name, for example, F:. Windows reroutes any request for data on the F drive to the file server.

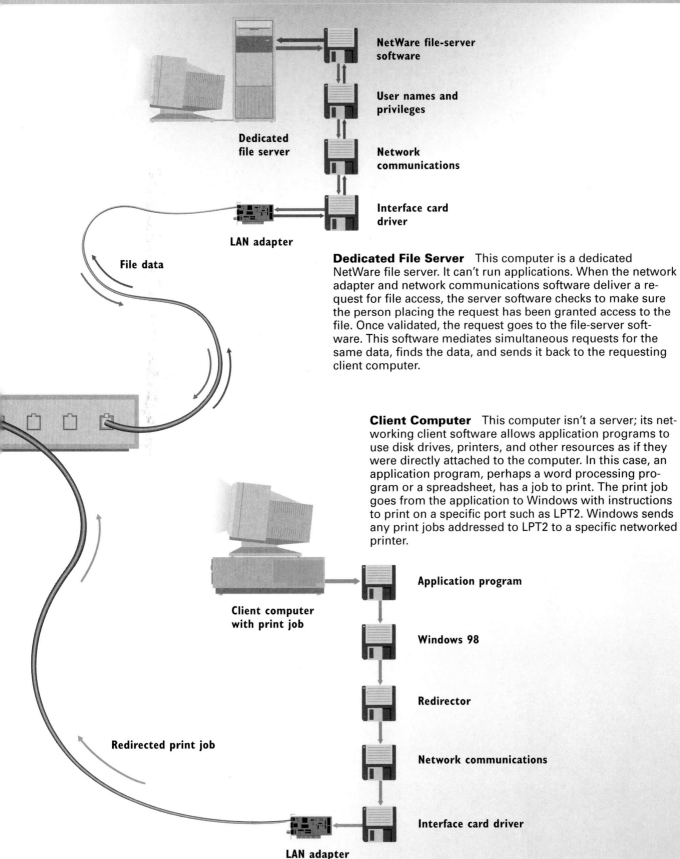

NetWare file-server
software

User names and
privileges

Network
communications

Interface card
driver

**Dedicated
file server**

LAN adapter

File data

Dedicated File Server   This computer is a dedicated
NetWare file server. It can't run applications. When the network
adapter and network communications software deliver a request for file access, the server software checks to make sure
the person placing the request has been granted access to the
file. Once validated, the request goes to the file-server software. This software mediates simultaneous requests for the
same data, finds the data, and sends it back to the requesting
client computer.

Client Computer   This computer isn't a server; its networking client software allows application programs to
use disk drives, printers, and other resources as if they
were directly attached to the computer. In this case, an
application program, perhaps a word processing program or a spreadsheet, has a job to print. The print job
goes from the application to Windows with instructions
to print on a specific port such as LPT2. Windows sends
any print jobs addressed to LPT2 to a specific networked
printer.

**Client computer
with print job**

Application program

Windows 98

Redirector

Network communications

Interface card driver

Redirected print job

LAN adapter

Network Operating System Data Packaging

Network operating systems package requests from the keyboard and from applications in a succession of data envelopes for transmission across the network. In this example, Novell's NetWare packages a file request in an IPX packet, and the LAN adapter packages the IPX request into an Ethernet frame. Each data envelope contains its own addressing and error-control information.

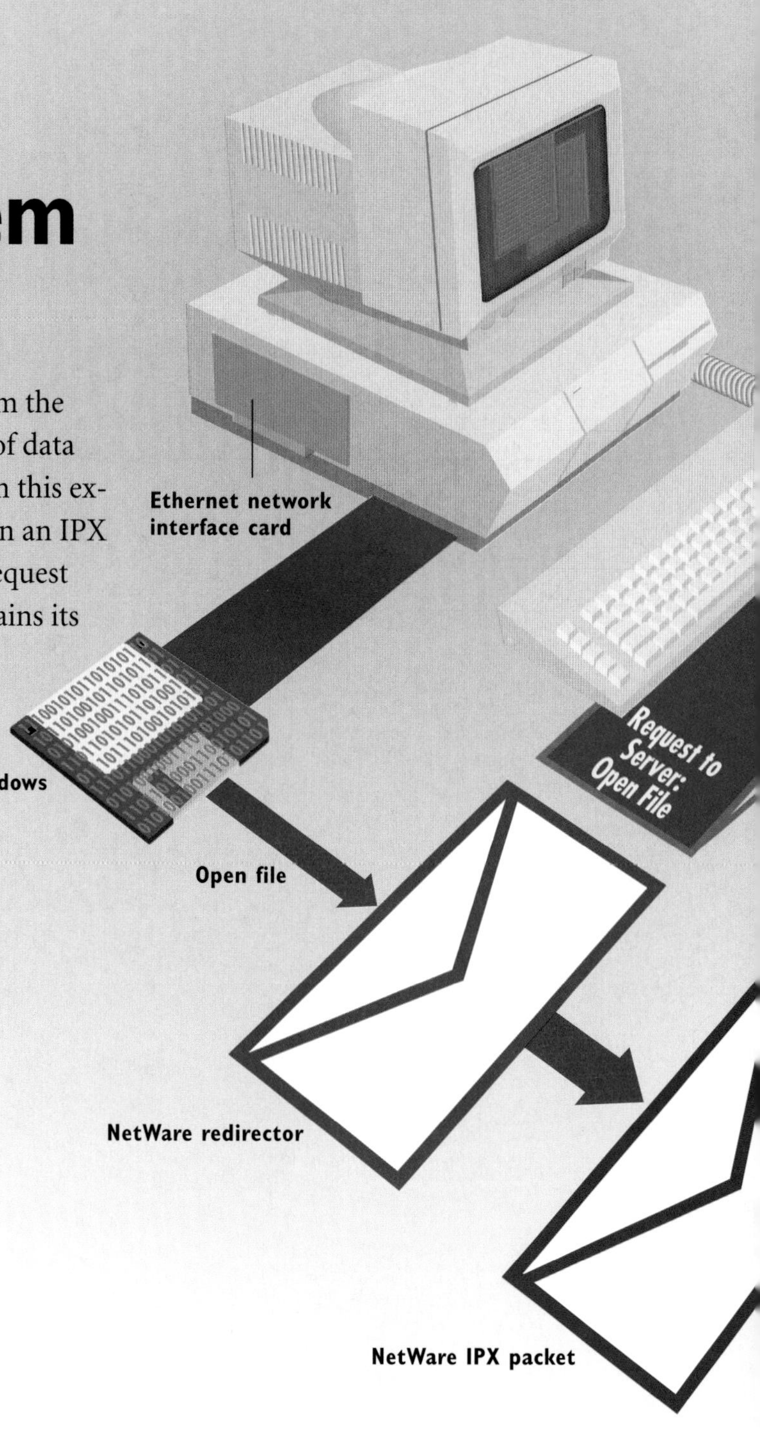

Ethernet network interface card

Windows

Request to Server: Open File

Open file

NetWare redirector

NetWare IPX packet

Keyboard entry: open file on F:

Data Field
Source Socket
Source Host
Source Network
Destination Source
Destination Host
Destination Network
Packet Type
Length
Error Control

Error Control
Data Field
Packet Length
Ethernet Source Address
Ethernet Destination Address
Synchronization Preamble

Ethernet frame

CHAPTER

15

The Network Interface Card

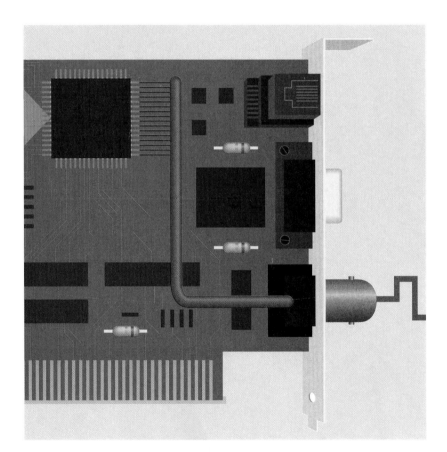

THE network interface card, or LAN adapter, functions as an interface between the computer and the network cabling, so it must serve two masters. Inside the computer, it moves data to and from the random-access memory (RAM). Outside the computer, it controls the flow of data in and out of the network cable system. An interface card has a specialized port that matches the electrical signaling standards used on the cable and the specific type of cable connector. In between the computer and the cable, the interface card must buffer the data, because the computer is typically much faster than the network. The interface card also must change the form of the data from a wide parallel stream coming in 8 bits at a time to a narrow stream moving 1 bit at a time in and out of the network port.

You must select a network interface card that matches your computer's data bus and the network cable. The Peripheral Component Interface (PCI) bus has emerged as a new standard for adapter card interfaces. PCI, originally associated with Intel Pentium computers, is now appearing in many systems. We suggest buying PCI-equipped computers and using PCI LAN adapters whenever possible.

PCI adapters can use a technique called *bus-mastering*, a more efficient method of moving data to and from the computer's memory. Bus-mastering lightens the load on the computer's processor by moving data to and from the computer's RAM without interrupting the processor, but this technique requires more processing power on the adapter board so these boards cost more.

PC Card adapters, formerly known as PCMCIA, slide into thin slots—typically in laptop computers. Despite its radically different physical form, a PC Card LAN adapter is practically identical electrically to an ISA-bus adapter.

On the network cable side, the LAN adapter performs three important functions: It generates the electrical signals that travel over the network cable; it follows specific rules controlling access to the cable; and it makes the physical connection to the cable. Adapters for Ethernet and Token-Ring both use the same basic system of electrical signaling over the cable. Surprisingly, the signals on these high-speed computer cables aren't very different from the early Morse code or Baudot teletype code. A technique called Manchester encoding provides a way to transmit 0's and 1's using direct current voltage pulses that range from −15 to +15 volts. The LAN adapters translate each change in the voltage level as a character in the ASCII data alphabet.

The technique the adapters use to control access to the cable and the type of cable connectors are attributes of the network architecture, such as Ethernet or Token-Ring, that you choose. We'll describe network architectures more thoroughly in the next chapter, but you should know that you will need adapters with the right connectors and the right protocols for access into the network cable.

Network Interface Card

A network interface card, or LAN adapter, uses a specialized processor and routines stored in read-only memory to move data to and from the computer's memory over the parallel data bus and to transmit and receive data on the serial network cable. It rearranges and buffers the data while handling the interface to the computer and the interface to the cable.

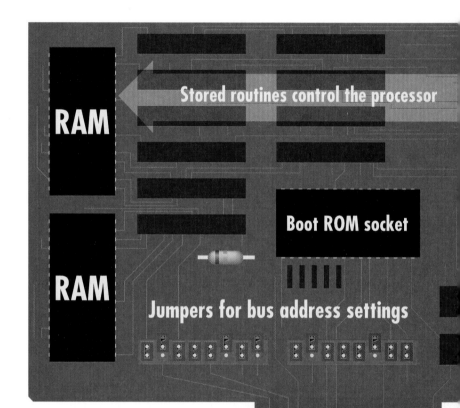

RAM

Stored routines control the processor

RAM

Boot ROM socket

Jumpers for bus address settings

Expansion bus connectors

Parallel data to and from the PC's memory over the expansion bus

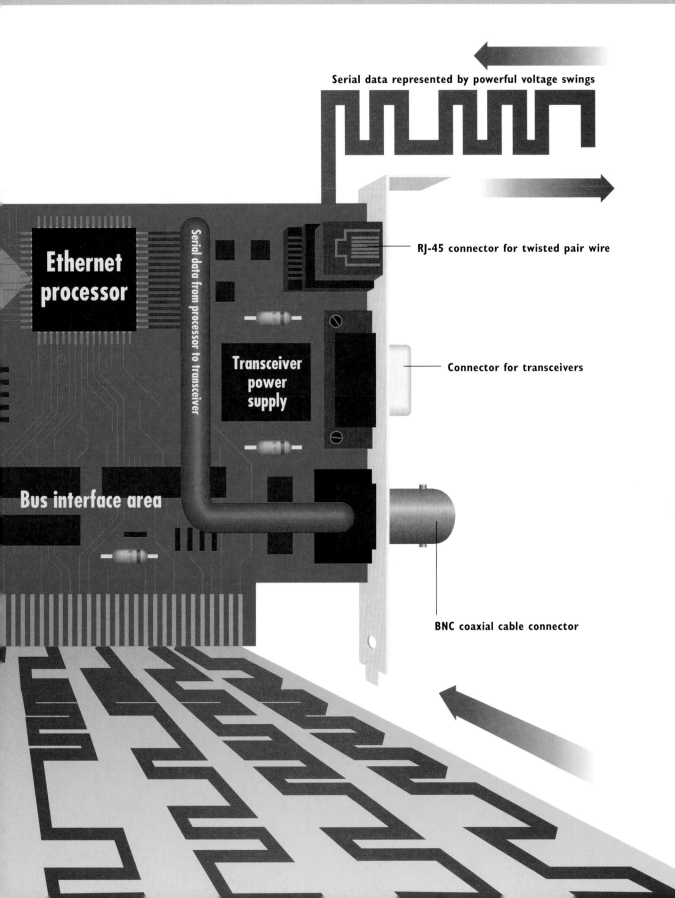

Serial data represented by powerful voltage swings

Ethernet processor

Serial data from processor to transceiver

RJ-45 connector for twisted pair wire

Transceiver power supply

Connector for transceivers

Bus interface area

BNC coaxial cable connector

PC Cards

PC Card LAN adapters slide into a thin slot—typically in laptop computers. The PC Card slot gives the adapter high-speed access to the processor and memory. The devices vary widely in how they connect to the LAN cable, so choose products with a durable connector. PC Card LAN adapters can be combined with modems and other devices to give more utility to the slot.

Bus interface

RAM

RAM

Ethernet processor

Cable interface

CHAPTER

16

Network Cabling

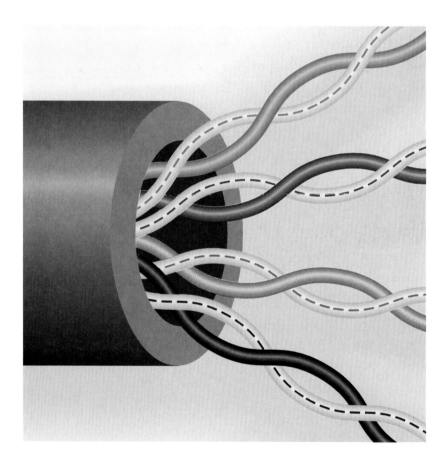

THE network interface cards and network operating system can't work without reliable and high-quality connections between the network nodes. When you select your network cabling, you face an array of standards and options. ARCnet, Ethernet, and Token-Ring are the three most commonly accepted sets of standards for controlling network signaling, cable access, and cable configurations. However, a new set of standards for cabling has emerged that overrides the cable standards established previously within each networking scheme. In the following pages, we'll illustrate the classic wiring configurations associated with each scheme as well as a new structured wiring system; we'll also examine LAN cable standards and wireless networking.

The network cable, or *media* as it's called in LAN-speak, is a single thread of copper or glass that links all the nodes on the network, but it can only carry the signals from one network interface card at a time. Thus each LAN architecture needs a media-access control (MAC) scheme so network interface cards can take turns transmitting into the cable.

In an Ethernet network, the interface cards share the common cable by listening before they transmit and transmitting only during a break in the traffic when the channel is quiet, a technique called *carrier-sense multiple access with collision detection* (CSMA/CD). With collision detection, if two stations begin to transmit at the same time, they detect the collision, stop, and retry after a sufficient time interval.

Token-Ring network interface cards use a much more complex media-access control scheme called *token-passing*. Ethernet cards contend for access to the cable; Token-Ring cards must have permission to transmit into a cable system that forms a complete electrical loop or ring. Under this technique, the active cards negotiate, using their built-in serial numbers, to determine a master interface card. The master initiates a special message called a free token. When an interface card with data to send receives a free token, it changes the free token into a message and sends it to the next station up the ring for relay. After the addressed interface card receives the message and the message returns to the originating interface card, that card initiates a new free token and the process begins again.

ARCnet network interface cards use a somewhat similar media-access control scheme. A master card, designated by the lowest number set into the cards through switches, maintains a table of all active cards and polls each one in turn, giving permission to transmit.

Network interface cards, also called LAN adapters, provide a wide variety of physical connections for the network cables. The trappings on the cables range from shiny metal Ethernet T-connectors to the simple plastic modular plugs used with unshielded twisted pair (UTP) wire.

Some Ethernet cards have connectors for coaxial cable, and others provide a 15-pin socket for more complex external transceivers for fiber optic and other types of cables. Token-Ring cards have a 9-pin connector for shielded twisted pair (STP) wire. However, unshielded twisted pair wire is becoming increasingly popular for both Token-Ring and Ethernet cards. These cards have a simple plastic rectangular jack similar to those found on modern telephones.

Modern network cable installations conform to specifications for structured wiring systems issued by the Electronic Industries Association and Underwriters' Laboratories. This architecture uses wire without an external shield of copper braid, but each pair of wires is twisted together at about six turns per inch. The twisting cancels electric currents—absorbed from power cables and other outside sources—that can mask the network signals. Structured wiring systems improve reliability by using dedicated spans of wire from each node to a central wiring hub. The hub automatically disconnects malfunctioning interface cards and defective wire spans so they don't degrade the rest of the network.

UTP cable systems are graded according to categories that describe the quality of the components and the installation techniques. Category 5 denotes the highest quality. We strongly suggest using only Category 5 materials and standards for all installations. Even the smallest networks will probably expand and need the firm foundation provided by a Category 5 UTP installation.

Some specialized network interface cards do not use copper cables. They can read pulses of laser light sent over fiber optic cables, pulses of invisible infrared light sent through the air, and signals imposed on radio waves. Modern installations often use copper cables for most connections and intermix fiber optic or wireless alternatives to reach special nodes.

LAN cables come in many physical configurations. Important selection considerations include resistance to *crosstalk*—electric currents between pairs of wires in the same cable—resistance to outside electrical fields caused by power lines, motors, relays, radio transmitters, and other devices; and ease of installation. If a cable resists internal and external electrical noise, network designers can use longer cables and faster signaling between nodes. Because fiber optic cables signal with pulses of light, they have total immunity from electrical noise. Fiber optic cables carry signals faster and farther than any other type of cable. Cables with outside shields of copper braid or foil, such as coaxial and shielded twisted pair, offer good resistance to electrical noise. But because they are thicker, they are difficult to pull through wiring conduits and walls. The thin unshielded twisted pair wire is easier to install, but it offers less resistance to electrical noise. Thin fiber optic cable doesn't fill conduits, but installers need special training and equipment to attach connectors, so the costs for fiber optic cable are high. As a final consideration, remember that the outer jackets of cables used inside air plenums and between floors must have special fire-resistant jackets to resist the spread of fire and the creation of toxic gas when exposed to flame.

Your network's operating system and even its network interface cards can be changed in a few hours or days. But changing the cabling requires weeks of work. Cable selection and installation are important steps in designing a network that will serve you economically and reliably for years. Study the options and carefully specify your needs.

Unshielded Twisted Pair (UTP) Wire

This cable typically combines four pairs of wires inside the same outer jacket. Each pair is twisted with a different number of twists per inch. The twisting cancels out electrical noise from adjacent pairs and from other devices in the building such as motors, relays, and transformers. Although unshielded twisted pair externally resembles common telephone wire, telephone wire lacks the twisting and other electrical characteristics needed to carry data.

SPEED & THROUGHPUT

AVERAGED COST PER NODE

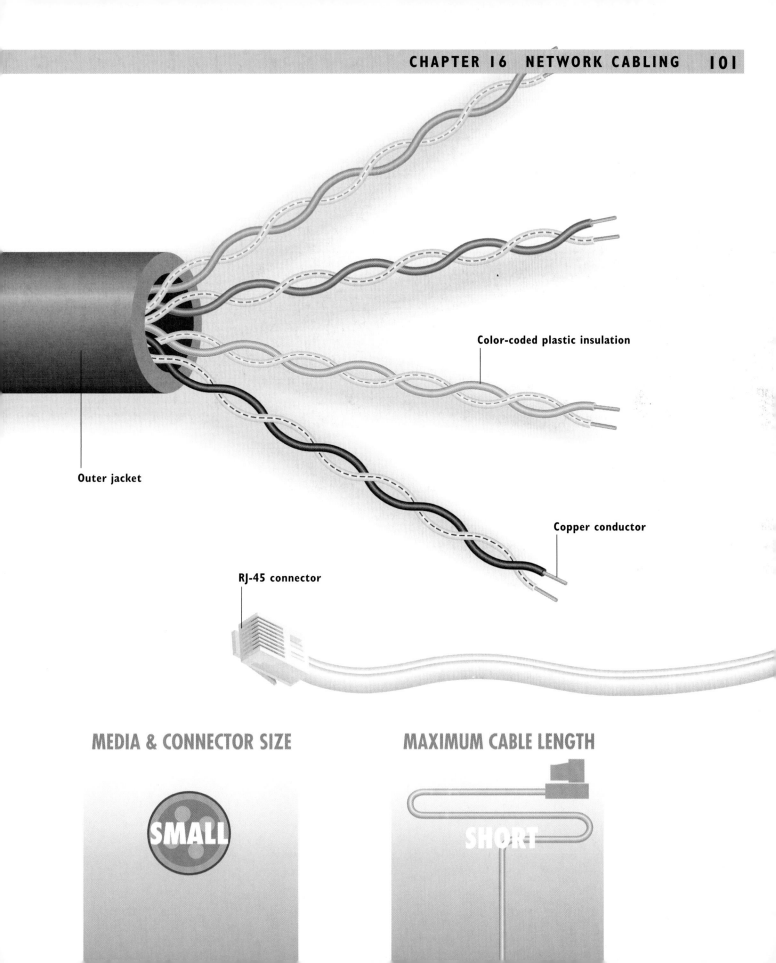

Color-coded plastic insulation

Outer jacket

Copper conductor

RJ-45 connector

MEDIA & CONNECTOR SIZE

SMALL

MAXIMUM CABLE LENGTH

SHORT

Coaxial Cable

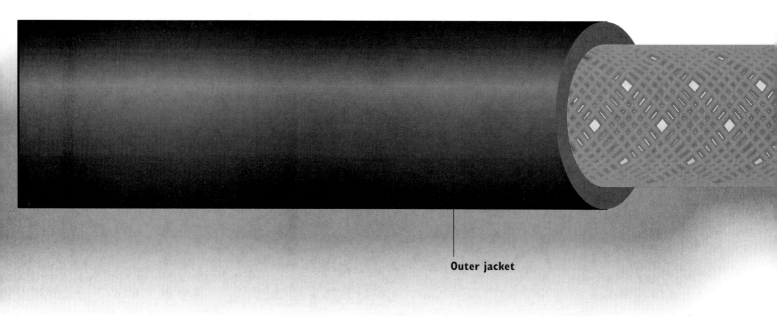

Outer jacket

This cable gets its name from the two conductors that share the same center axis; they are coaxial. Coaxial cable relies on woven copper braid to shield the center conductor from outside electric currents. The Ethernet and ARCnet specifications both include coaxial cable, but they each call for a different type of cable.

SPEED & THROUGHPUT

FAST ENOUGH

AVERAGED COST PER NODE

INEXPENSIVE

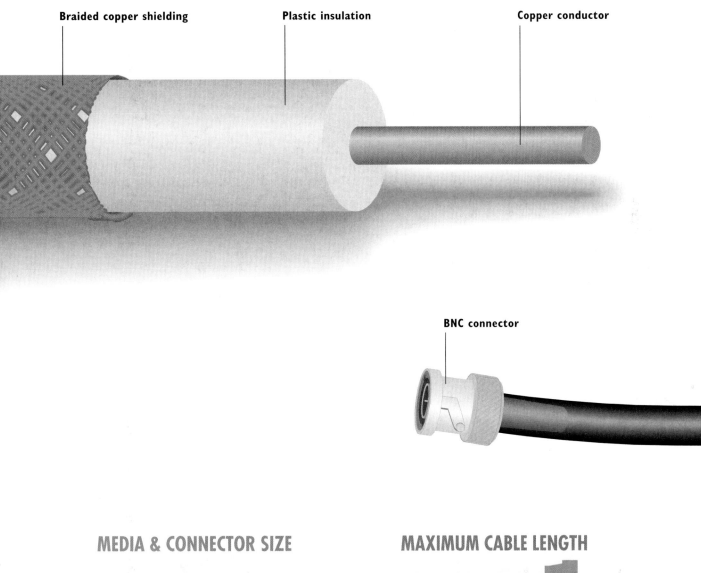

Braided copper shielding

Plastic insulation

Copper conductor

BNC connector

MEDIA & CONNECTOR SIZE

MEDIUM

MAXIMUM CABLE LENGTH

MEDIUM

Shielded Twisted Pair (STP) Wire

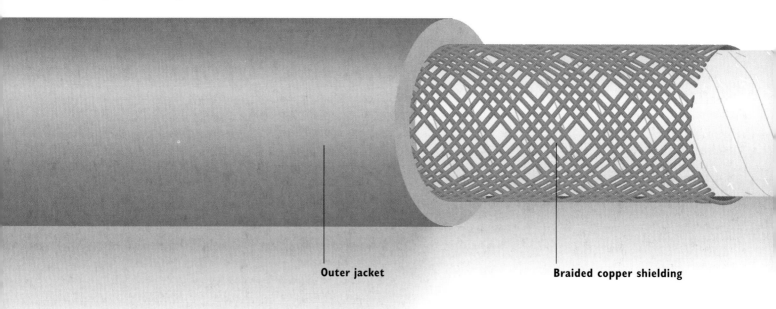

Outer jacket

Braided copper shielding

This cable, called for only in the Token-Ring LAN specifications, uses a woven copper braid, a foil wrap between and around the wire pairs, and internal twisting of the pairs to provide a high degree of protection from outside electric currents. However, the combination creates a thick cable that rapidly fills the space in building wiring ducts.

SPEED & THROUGHPUT

VERY FAST

AVERAGED COST PER NODE

EXPENSIVE

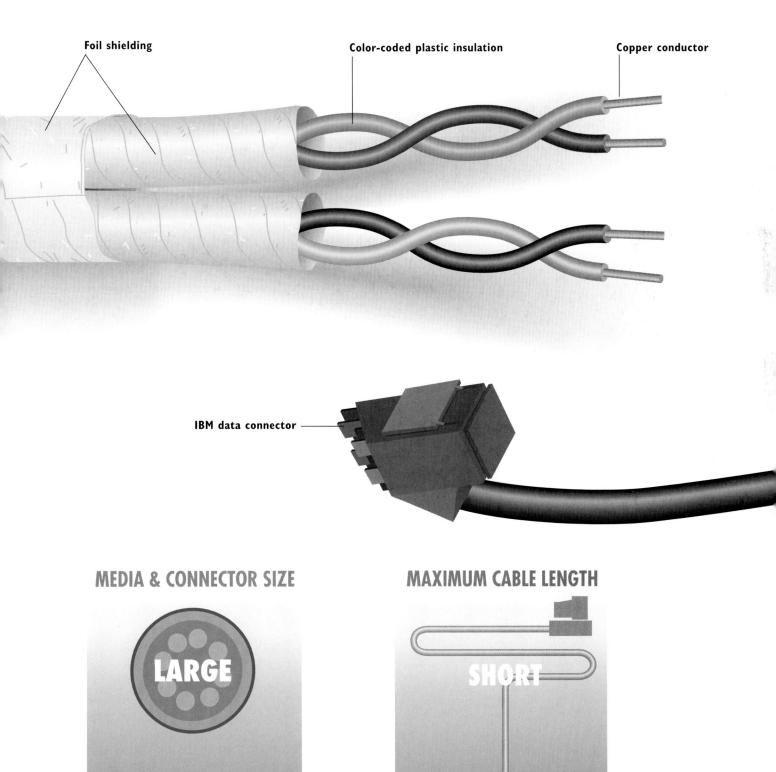

Foil shielding

Color-coded plastic insulation

Copper conductor

IBM data connector

MEDIA & CONNECTOR SIZE

LARGE

MAXIMUM CABLE LENGTH

SHORT

Fiber-Optic Cable

Outer jacket

Because the signals it carries are pulses of light conducted over threads of glass, fiber-optic cables aren't bothered by outside electric currents. Each glass strand only passes signals in one direction, so a cable has two strands in separate jackets. Each jacket has a group of Kevlar fibers for strength, and a reinforcing layer of plastic surrounds the glass strand. Special connectors make an optically pure connection to the glass fiber and provide a window for laser transmitters and optical receivers. Because they are free of interference and the light pulses travel for miles without losing appreciable strength, fiber-optic cables can carry data at high signaling speeds over long distances.

SPEED & THROUGHPUT

FASTEST POSSIBLE

AVERAGED COST PER NODE

MOST EXPENSIVE

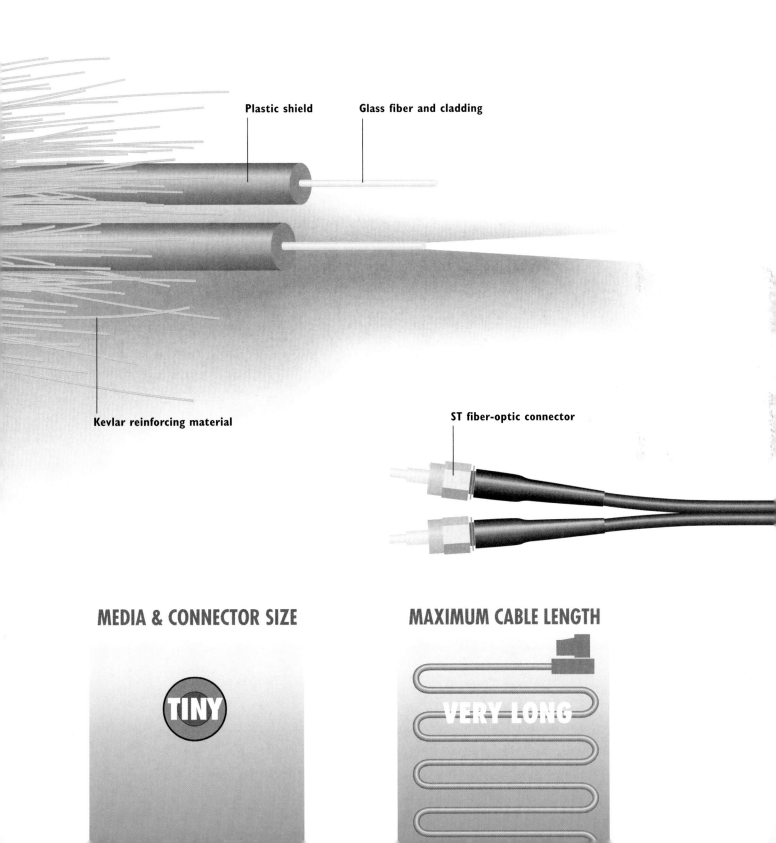

Plastic shield

Glass fiber and cladding

Kevlar reinforcing material

ST fiber-optic connector

MEDIA & CONNECTOR SIZE

TINY

MAXIMUM CABLE LENGTH

VERY LONG

Ethernet Networking

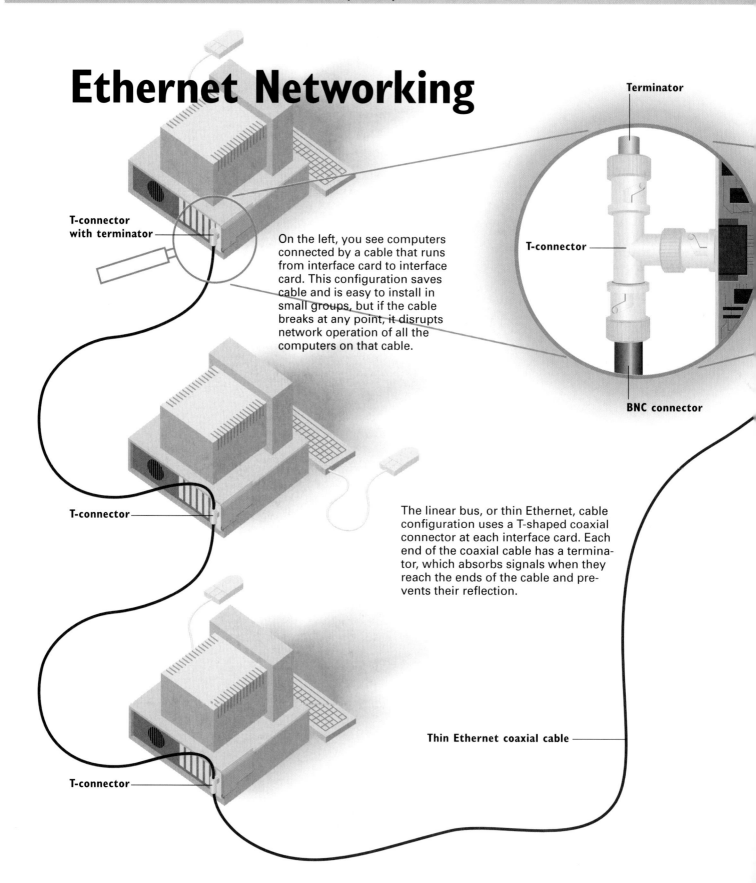

Terminator

T-connector

BNC connector

T-connector with terminator

On the left, you see computers connected by a cable that runs from interface card to interface card. This configuration saves cable and is easy to install in small groups, but if the cable breaks at any point, it disrupts network operation of all the computers on that cable.

T-connector

The linear bus, or thin Ethernet, cable configuration uses a T-shaped coaxial connector at each interface card. Each end of the coaxial cable has a terminator, which absorbs signals when they reach the ends of the cable and prevents their reflection.

Thin Ethernet coaxial cable

T-connector

Although network interface cards usually reside in computer expansion slots, you can connect to computers that don't have slots, such as laptops, using an external network interface card. You can choose from adapters with coaxial or unshielded twisted pair wire connectors.

External network interface card

Wiring hub

A wiring hub provides a central point for the cables attached to each network interface card. You can select hubs with connectors for coaxial, fiber optic, and twisted pair wire. In this example, the hub connects to the thin Ethernet linear bus of coaxial cable and has a strip of connectors for unshielded twisted pair wire.

Unshielded twisted pair wire used in 10BaseT, 100BaseT, and gigabit Ethernet configurations

RJ-45 connector

The Ethernet configuration using unshielded twisted pair wire is known as 10BaseT because it uses 10 megabit per second (Mbps) signaling speed, direct current, or baseband, signaling, and twisted pair wire. This configuration includes a central wiring hub with special circuitry to isolate malfunctioning segments of the network. Unshielded twisted pair wire uses a small plastic connector called an RJ-45 connector at each end of the wire. New signaling schemes such as 100BaseT and gigabit Ethernet use the same UTP cabling with upgraded hubs and adapters.

Token-Ring Network

This Token-Ring network has one network with two physically separate wiring hubs. The hubs, connected by fiber optic cable, can be thousands of feet apart. The computers and other networked devices, connected by either shielded or unshielded twisted pair wires, must be within approximately 100 feet of the wiring hub. The packages of data, called *frames*, move from node to node in a circle, but the wiring is in a star configuration. The actual ring in a Token-Ring network exists within the wiring hubs.

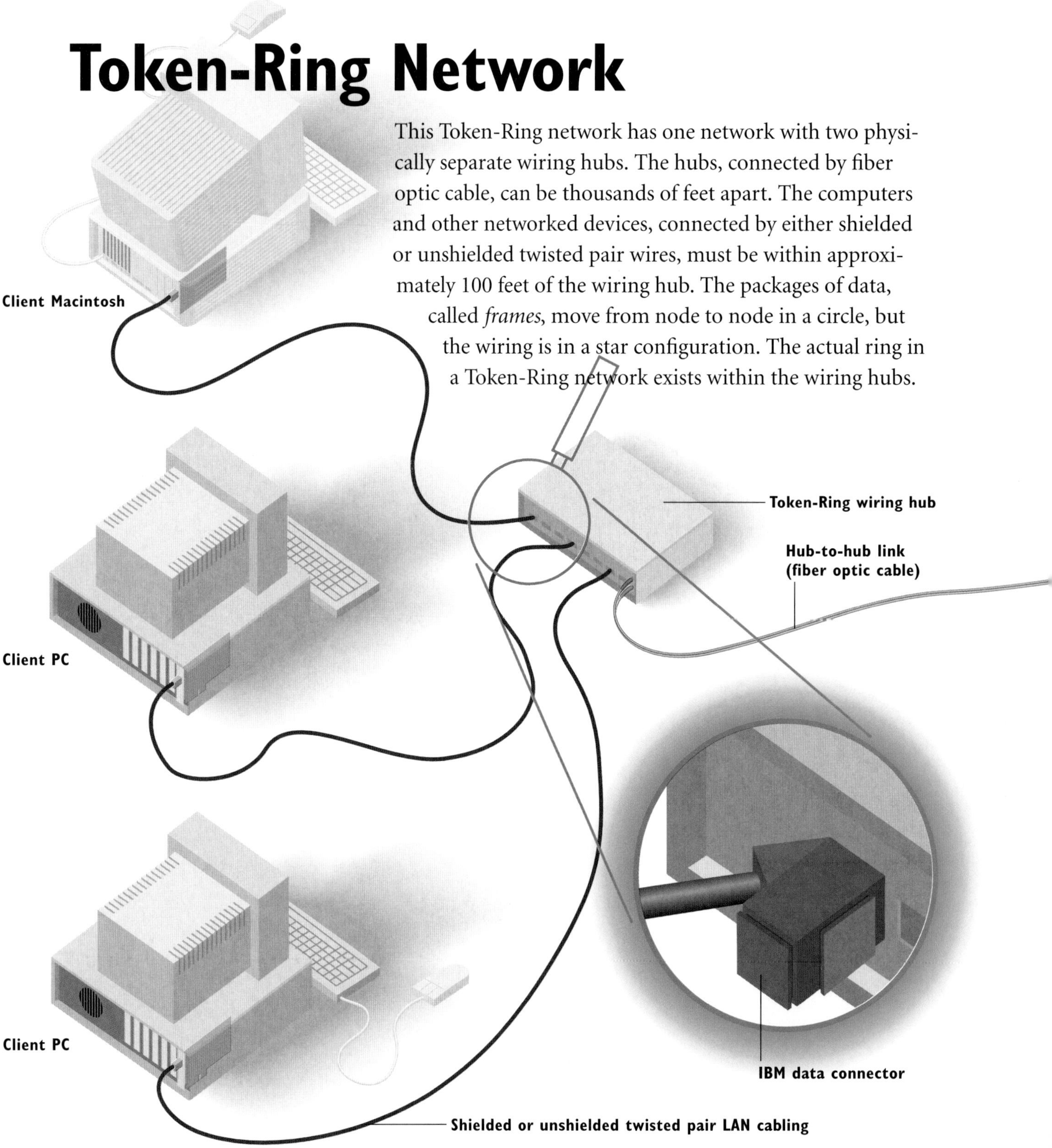

Client Macintosh

Token-Ring wiring hub

Hub-to-hub link (fiber optic cable)

Client PC

Client PC

IBM data connector

Shielded or unshielded twisted pair LAN cabling

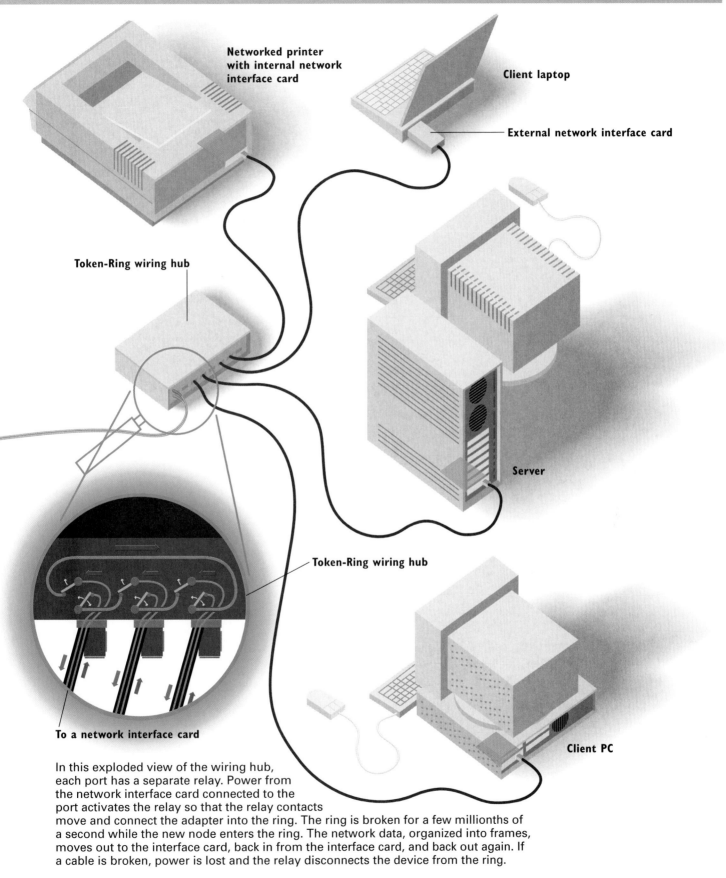

Networked printer with internal network interface card

Client laptop

External network interface card

Token-Ring wiring hub

Server

Token-Ring wiring hub

To a network interface card

Client PC

In this exploded view of the wiring hub, each port has a separate relay. Power from the network interface card connected to the port activates the relay so that the relay contacts move and connect the adapter into the ring. The ring is broken for a few millionths of a second while the new node enters the ring. The network data, organized into frames, moves out to the interface card, back in from the interface card, and back out again. If a cable is broken, power is lost and the relay disconnects the device from the ring.

Structured Wiring System

A structured wiring system provides a standardized way to wire a building for all types of networks. The main distribution frame links all the building's interior wiring and provides an interface connection to circuits coming from outside sources such as the local telephone company. Wiring hubs provide the connection logic unique to Ethernet, Token-Ring, or ARCnet adapters.

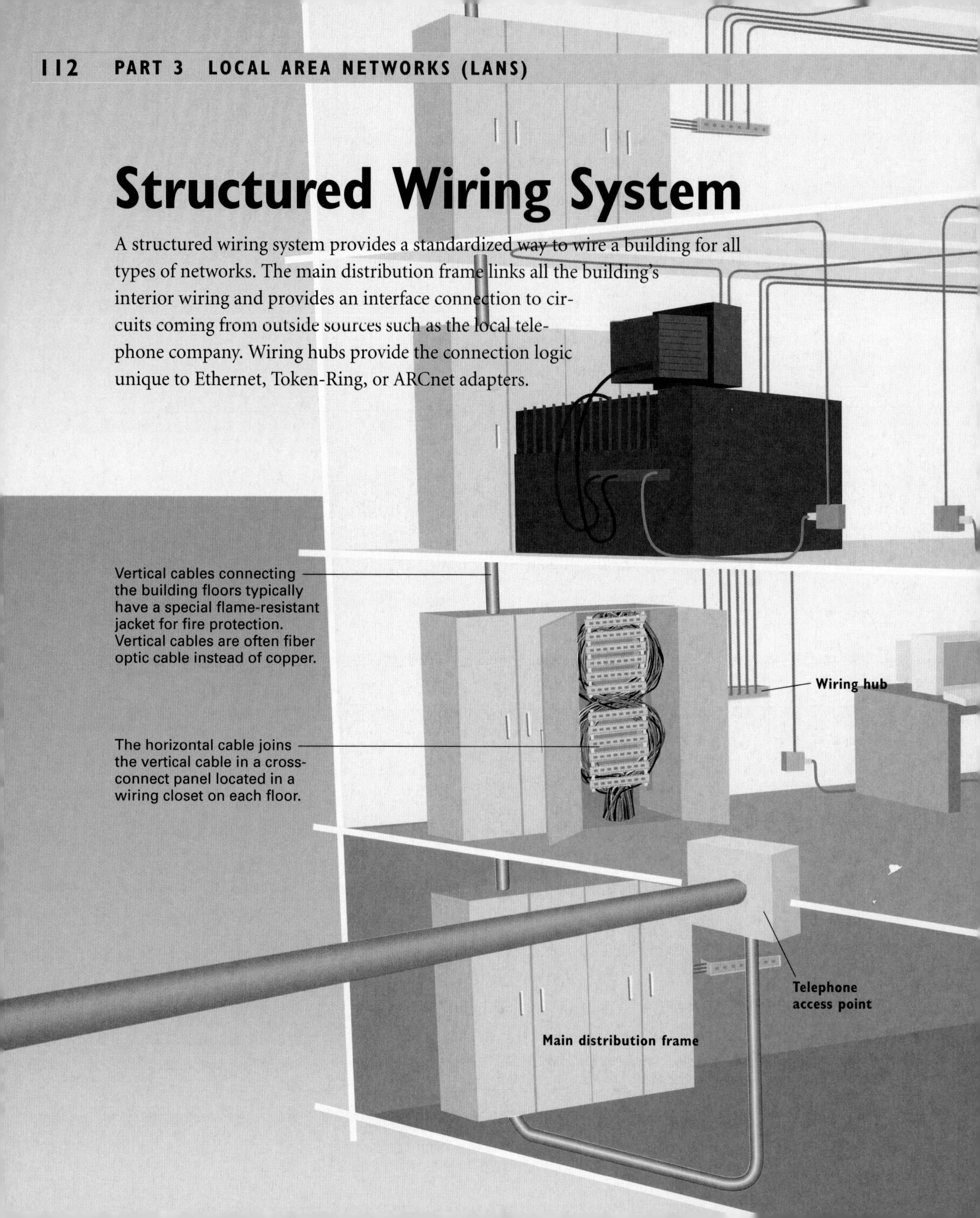

Vertical cables connecting the building floors typically have a special flame-resistant jacket for fire protection. Vertical cables are often fiber optic cable instead of copper.

The horizontal cable joins the vertical cable in a cross-connect panel located in a wiring closet on each floor.

Wiring hub

Telephone access point

Main distribution frame

Server

Each floor's horizontal cable—usually unshielded twisted pair copper wire—distributes the network connections to wall jacks near each piece of networked equipment.

Networked printer

Server

Wall plate

Wireless Networking

Some networked systems don't use any cables. Wireless network devices extend networks beyond the reach of copper or fiber optic cables. We categorize wireless network devices into those that work within a room or building, those that work across a city, and those that work around the world. Each type of product uses different technology and has different costs and operating speeds, but they all offer portable or mobile computing capability for people on the go.

Local wireless systems extend a wired network to laptop and palm-top computers within a room or building. Small wall-mounted transceivers connect to the wired LAN and establish radio contact with portable networked devices within their broadcast range.

11:00 - Status Report Meeting: OMRI (more)

1:30 - Late lunch with new Ad Agency (more)

3:00 - Call Printing Company, Inc. > Mr. Davis

4:00 - Call daycare > Mrs. Elwain

4:30 - FAX Melinda re: final changes 17.6 (more)

90 - Download iNET:email:MTDwork (auto)

Dinner with Laurie N (more)

Michael's PDA STATUS

Cellular Link: OPEN

Fax/Modem: IDLE

Battery: 67%

Processor: 100%

Compression: ON

Sound: ON

csimile recieved from N. Voskuil

: data available for review

mpressed & ready for review

6.11.94   2:47pm

Wireless adapters using cellular telephone technology connect portable and mobile computers scattered across a wide area into their local networks. Small antennas on the back of or within personal computers communicate with radio towers in the surrounding area.

Wireless networking around the world uses satellites in near-earth orbit that can pick up low-powered signals from portable and mobile networked devices.

Cellular Wireless

Cellular data communications use the cellular telephone network to carry data between a mobile PC or terminal and a host computer

Limit of call coverage

1 The cellular telephone network uses 800 MHz radio signals to communicate between the cellular service provider and a customer's cellular phone. The cellular phone company operates a network of radio receivers and transmitters called *sites*. Cell sites are typically located a few miles apart, usually on towers about 150 feet tall. Many cellular systems offer a choice between digital and analog service. Digital cellular is typically more reliable and has better audio quality than the older analog service, and is better suited for cellular modem communications. While digital cell phones are typically more expensive than their analog counterparts, the monthly service is often less expensive than analog.

2 Each cell site can support dozens of users at one time, and the cell sites are carefully placed so that each cell site's coverage overlaps its neighboring sites' coverage area. The area of coverage provided by each site is called a *cell*.

Radio tower

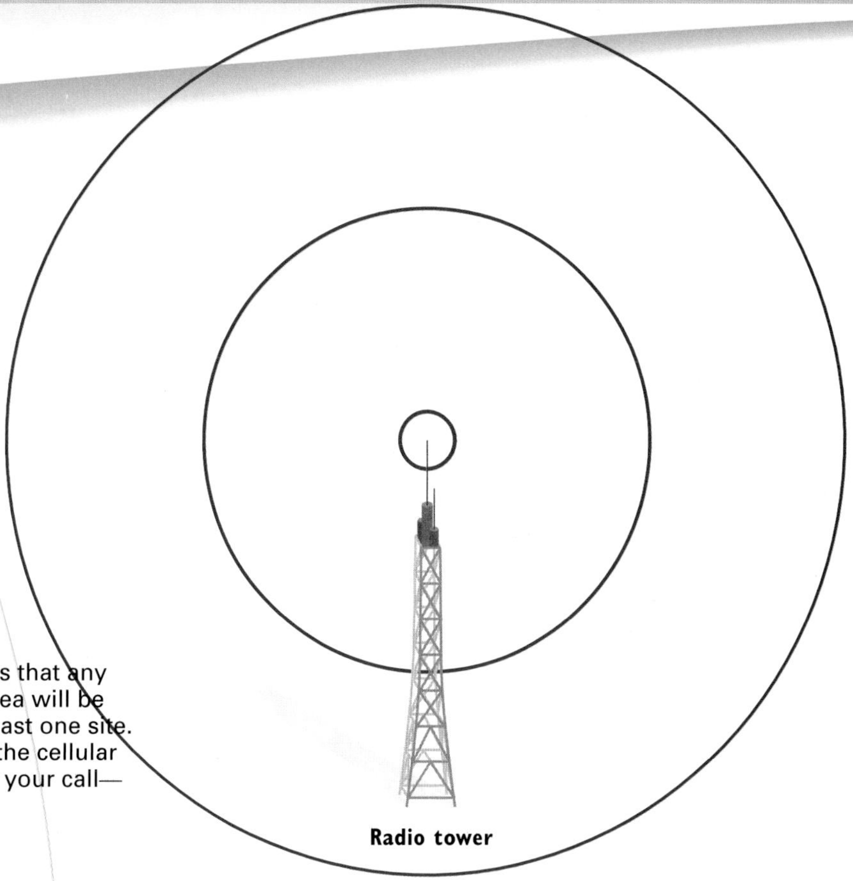

3 The overlap of the cells ensures that any phone traveling through the area will be able to communicate with at least one site. As you move from cell to cell, the cellular system automatically switches your call—a process called *handing off*.

Radio tower

4 Cellular data communications require a cellular telephone and a special cellular modem. Most cellular modems are PC Cards designed to fit into laptop computers. The modem attaches to the cell phone via a cable. Cell modems are similar to regular modems, except that they are more tolerant of noisy and interrupted connections—a common problem with cellular telephones.

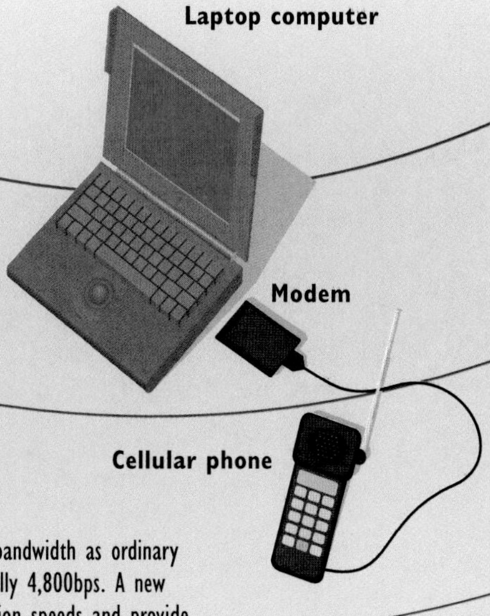

Laptop computer

Modem

Limit of call coverage

Cellular phone

NOTE Cellular phone connections don't have as much bandwidth as ordinary phone lines, so cellular modems run at slower speeds—typically 4,800bps. A new breed of digital cellular phones promises to increase transmission speeds and provide more reliable communications, but requires users to buy a new phone and modem.

CHAPTER

17

Server-Based LANs

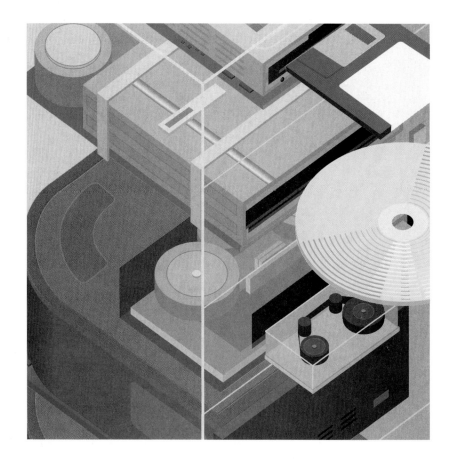

THERE are four types of servers—file servers, print servers, application servers, and communications servers—but under different network strategies various devices on the network can also perform these server functions. One network strategy relies on a single powerful computer that is dedicated to providing all server functions for dozens or even hundreds of client computers on the network. This is known as *server-based networking.*

Another network strategy, known as *peer-to-peer networking*, distributes the server functions among many computers. They act as file or print servers even while they run application programs such as spreadsheets and databases. We'll describe the pros and cons of peer-to-peer networking in the next chapter.

Server-based networks have a higher start-up cost than peer-to-peer networks and, typically, require more technical expertise to install and manage because of the powerful hardware and software they use. But this strategy benefits from economy of scale; as you install more client computers that share the server's resources, a server-based network becomes more economical.

A computer designed to act as a dedicated file server has cabinet space for more disk drives, a bigger power supply to handle the load, the ability to expand to hundreds of megabytes of RAM, a fast interface bus, and the fastest affordable processor. It isn't unusual to find a dedicated server equipped with several network interface cards. Each card addresses a separate segment of cabling so that the data-carrying capacity of a single cable doesn't block the use of the server's power.

Server-based systems provide good control, backup, and management of critical data because important records and files reside in one place. The file server runs a multitasking operating system that can execute several programs at the same time, so, while it is saving or opening a file, the server can also record the date and time of the action, check for computer viruses, and flag the file for backup to a tape drive. Management reports from the server software can help network administrators spot the need for more resources, such as disk-drive storage. Server software can even bill individuals and departments for use of the server's resources.

Powerful server-based networks offer security, excellent data management, fast response, and room for expansion. But they are complex and represent a considerable investment in equipment, software, and training.

Server-Based LANs

A large and powerful computer is the heart of a server-based network. The networked client computers use the file, print, and communications services of the central server. This architecture is robust, powerful, complex, and has a significant installation cost, but as you add more users, the cost-per-user drops.

Client computers

Each client computer runs its own application programs, and networking software in each client computer redirects requests for file and print services to the file server. Files created by the applications, and perhaps the application programs themselves, cross the network from the file server. This network uses several parallel network cable runs to ensure that the client computers can benefit from the fast data handling of the server.

This computer, designed to act as a central server, is equipped with multiple hard disk drives, a tape drive for backup, and a CD-ROM drive. It uses a specialized multitasking operating system and runs a variety of management and monitoring programs, in addition to the file and print services.

How Thin Network Clients Work

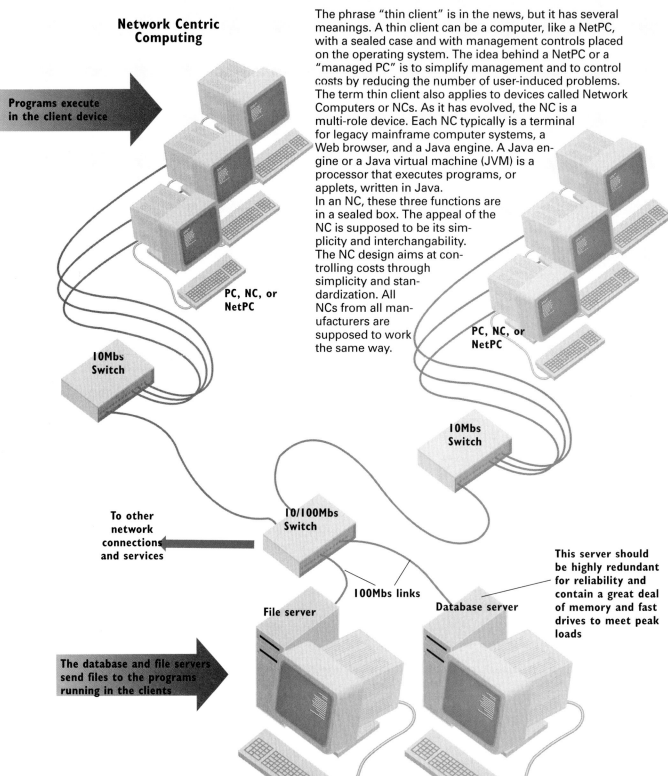

Network Centric Computing

Programs execute in the client device

PC, NC, or NetPC

10Mbs Switch

The phrase "thin client" is in the news, but it has several meanings. A thin client can be a computer, like a NetPC, with a sealed case and with management controls placed on the operating system. The idea behind a NetPC or a "managed PC" is to simplify management and to control costs by reducing the number of user-induced problems. The term thin client also applies to devices called Network Computers or NCs. As it has evolved, the NC is a multi-role device. Each NC typically is a terminal for legacy mainframe computer systems, a Web browser, and a Java engine. A Java engine or a Java virtual machine (JVM) is a processor that executes programs, or applets, written in Java.
In an NC, these three functions are in a sealed box. The appeal of the NC is supposed to be its simplicity and interchangability. The NC design aims at controlling costs through simplicity and standardization. All NCs from all manufacturers are supposed to work the same way.

PC, NC, or NetPC

10Mbs Switch

To other network connections and services

10/100Mbs Switch

100Mbs links

File server

Database server

This server should be highly redundant for reliability and contain a great deal of memory and fast drives to meet peak loads

The database and file servers send files to the programs running in the clients

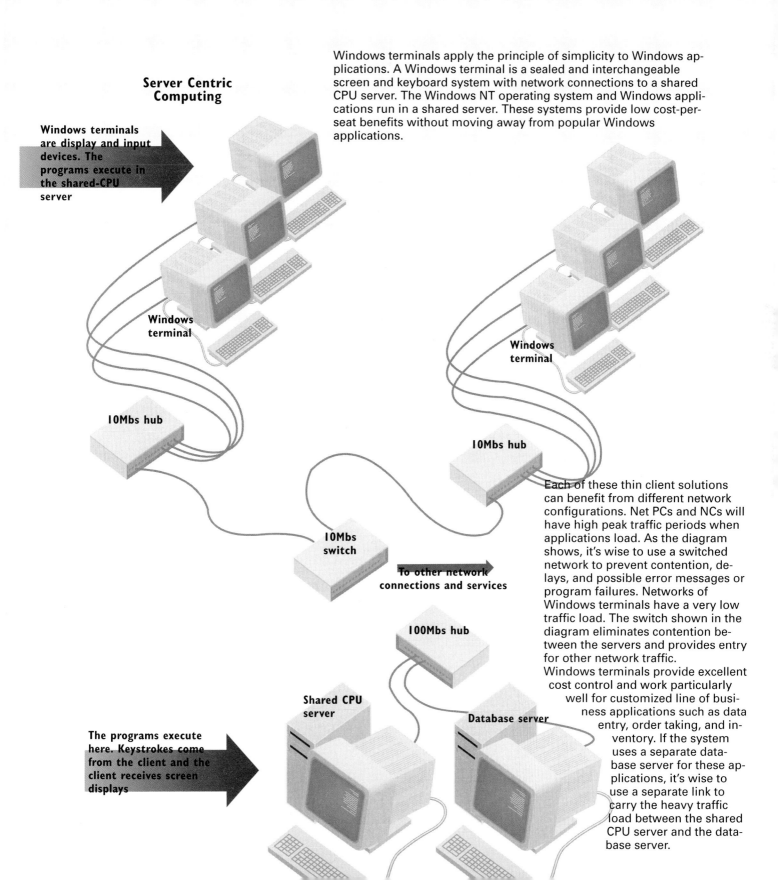

Server Centric Computing

Windows terminals apply the principle of simplicity to Windows applications. A Windows terminal is a sealed and interchangeable screen and keyboard system with network connections to a shared CPU server. The Windows NT operating system and Windows applications run in a shared server. These systems provide low cost-per-seat benefits without moving away from popular Windows applications.

Windows terminals are display and input devices. The programs execute in the shared-CPU server

Windows terminal

Windows terminal

10Mbs hub

10Mbs hub

10Mbs switch

To other network connections and services

100Mbs hub

Shared CPU server

Database server

The programs execute here. Keystrokes come from the client and the client receives screen displays

Each of these thin client solutions can benefit from different network configurations. Net PCs and NCs will have high peak traffic periods when applications load. As the diagram shows, it's wise to use a switched network to prevent contention, delays, and possible error messages or program failures. Networks of Windows terminals have a very low traffic load. The switch shown in the diagram eliminates contention between the servers and provides entry for other network traffic.

Windows terminals provide excellent cost control and work particularly well for customized line of business applications such as data entry, order taking, and inventory. If the system uses a separate database server for these applications, it's wise to use a separate link to carry the heavy traffic load between the shared CPU server and the database server.

CHAPTER

18

Peer-to-Peer Networks

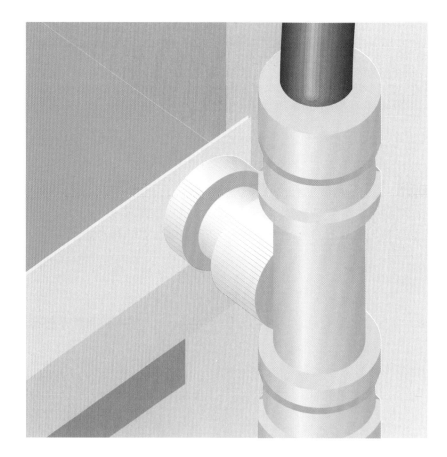

IN the last chapter, we described server-based networks that dedicate a computer to act as a file server, print server, and possibly as a communications server, too. In this chapter we'll describe the advantages and disadvantages of peer-to-peer networks, which don't rely on one dedicated server. This strategy shares the processing power and storage capacity of networked computers even while they run application programs.

Peer-to-peer networking makes sense because personal computers seem to defy the laws of supply and demand—their power goes up while their prices go down or at least stay the same. Modern desktop computers have power to spare and to share, so if they are not used heavily to run applications, they become even more valuable as file and print servers. Peer-to-peer networking offers excellent economy because it takes advantage of computer hardware that's already paid for.

In a peer-to-peer network, some computers run file-server networking software in addition to client networking software, application programs, and an underlying operating system. This type of peer-to-peer networking software is a part of the Macintosh operating environment and Microsoft's Windows family of products. However, just because server software is present, a computer's resources are not automatically open to everyone on the network. The person using a particular computer decides what files, subdirectories, or drives are shared across the network. Peer-to-peer network operating systems make it easy to share devices—such as CD-ROM drives, tape drives, and removable cartridge drives—with any other networked computer.

Peer-to-peer network operating systems typically don't have the powerful management and auditing features found in server-based software because that processing power is used by local applications. However, they are easy to install and maintain and provide good responsiveness—particularly if the file read and write load is shared among several computers acting as file servers. It's also possible to combine peer-to-peer networking with a server-based architecture.

Peer-to-peer networks offer a low start-up cost, simplicity, and enough power to satisfy the needs of many organizations.

Peer-to-Peer Networks

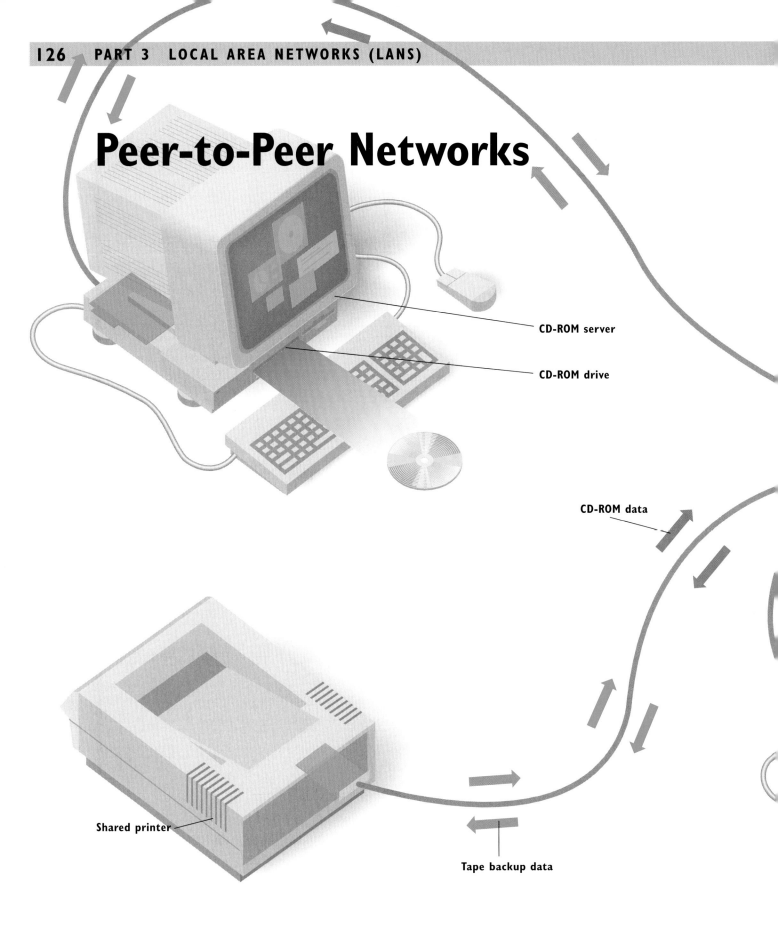

CD-ROM server

CD-ROM drive

CD-ROM data

Shared printer

Tape backup data

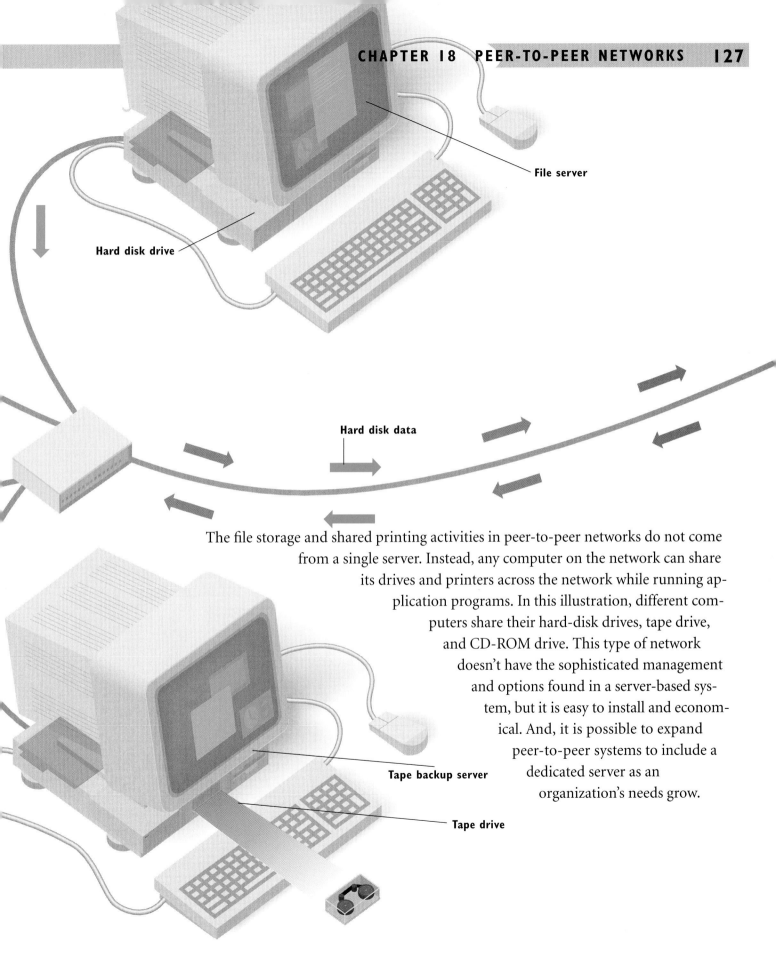

File server

Hard disk drive

Hard disk data

Tape backup server

Tape drive

The file storage and shared printing activities in peer-to-peer networks do not come from a single server. Instead, any computer on the network can share its drives and printers across the network while running application programs. In this illustration, different computers share their hard-disk drives, tape drive, and CD-ROM drive. This type of network doesn't have the sophisticated management and options found in a server-based system, but it is easy to install and economical. And, it is possible to expand peer-to-peer systems to include a dedicated server as an organization's needs grow.

CHAPTER

19

Enterprise Network Systems

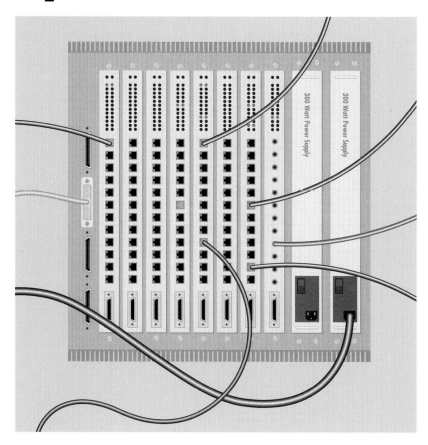

COMPUTER

COMPUTER networks have become the assembly line, warehouse, and delivery system for many organizations, so networks deserve all the management resources once lavished on the forges and furnaces of heavy industry. The primary technique for tracking the health of the corporate computer system is called *network management.*

Network management programs run in servers, in wiring hubs, and even on network interface cards. They gather statistics on the movement of data and watch for conditions that exceed programmed limits. If they detect a problem, they alert a central management program that can direct certain types of restart or rerouting actions and call for human assistance.

Manufacturers of network equipment have adopted several sets of standards for the operation of network management software. A popular set of standards, the Simple Network Management Protocols (SNMP), serves as a good example for all the systems. Under the SNMP architecture, small management programs, known as *agents*, run in special processors contained in a variety of networked devices. These programs monitor the devices and gather statistical data in a format known as a *management information base* (MIB, rhymes with *bib*). A central program, known as the *management console program*, polls the agents on a regular basis and downloads the contents of their MIBs.

A wiring hub is a very effective location for a management agent. The hub sits at the center of the wiring system, and the agent can monitor the level of activity and the type of data moving to and from each client and server. Servers often have their own agents that report more details on the condition of the server and on the actions of the client computers. Management agents are also available for certain models of network interface cards and for specialized products, such as uninterruptible power supplies with network attachments.

Management console programs use graphical maps and representations of the network. Their screens present marching bar graphs showing network traffic at the monitored points. These programs can also send detailed statistical data to database programs for analysis.

If the data coming in from the agents exceeds certain criteria, management console programs can even dial a telephone number and summon human help through a pager. The screen of the management console shows trouble spots with bold flashing colors. Network managers can use the management console to command changes in the network—typically at the wiring hubs.

A network management system adds to the cost of a network and isn't necessary in every organization. A network management system may start out with a little monitoring and reporting, typically from a wiring hub, and then more sophisticated capabilities can be added as needed. If a network is a vital part of an organization, then a network management system is inexpensive insurance for the success of the operation.

Network Management System

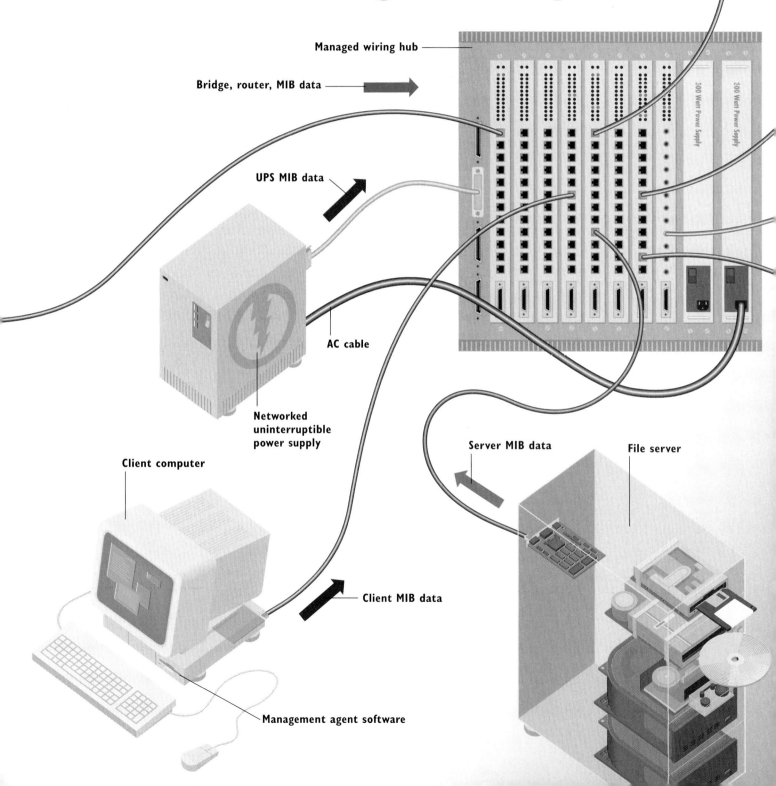

Managed wiring hub

Bridge, router, MIB data

UPS MIB data

AC cable

Networked
uninterruptible
power supply

Client computer

Client MIB data

Management agent software

Server MIB data

File server

300 Watt Power Supply

300 Watt Power Supply

A network management system uses programs called agents, which run in special processors installed in a variety of networked devices. These programs gather data in a format known as a management information base (MIB) and transfer it to a management console program running in a computer with a highly graphical display. The management console program creates network maps, bar charts, and other informative displays. The console software can automatically order some actions—for example, disconnecting a disruptive computer from the network and notifying a human operator of emergency conditions.

Wiring hub MIB data

Management console screen

Enterprise Networking

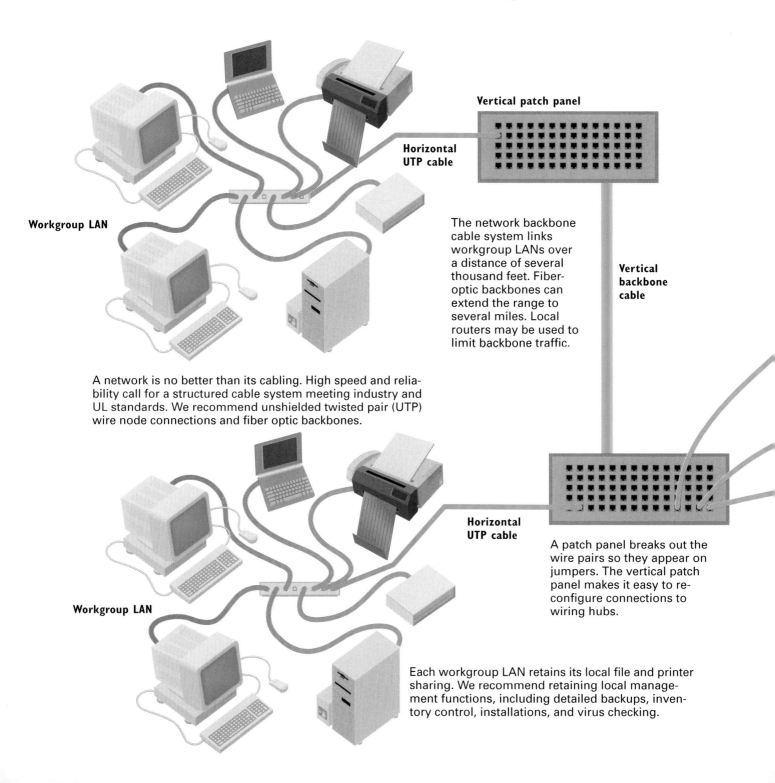

Vertical patch panel

Horizontal UTP cable

Workgroup LAN

The network backbone cable system links workgroup LANs over a distance of several thousand feet. Fiber-optic backbones can extend the range to several miles. Local routers may be used to limit backbone traffic.

Vertical backbone cable

A network is no better than its cabling. High speed and relia-bility call for a structured cable system meeting industry and UL standards. We recommend unshielded twisted pair (UTP) wire node connections and fiber optic backbones.

Horizontal UTP cable

A patch panel breaks out the wire pairs so they appear on jumpers. The vertical patch panel makes it easy to re-configure connections to wiring hubs.

Workgroup LAN

Each workgroup LAN retains its local file and printer sharing. We recommend retaining local manage-ment functions, including detailed backups, inven-tory control, installations, and virus checking.

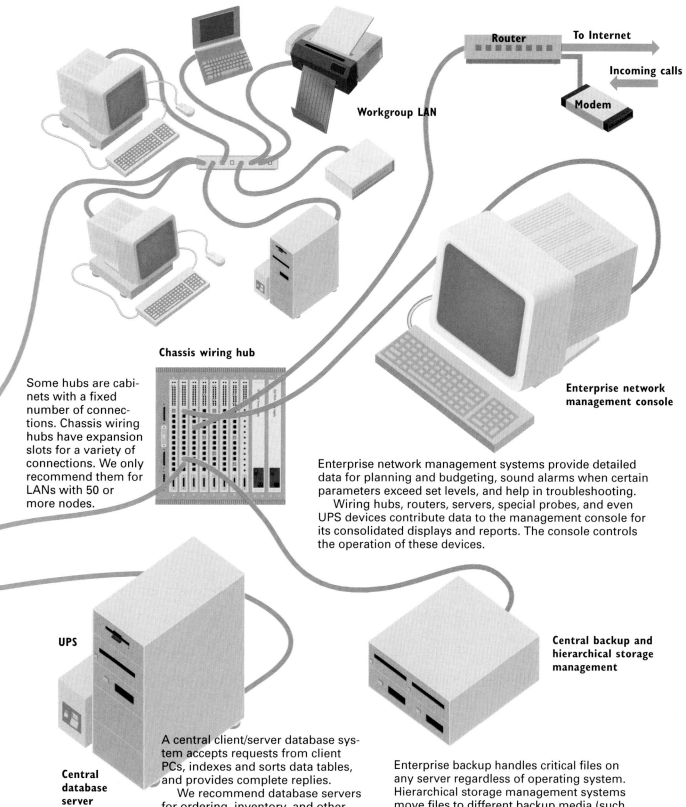

Workgroup LAN

Router

To Internet

Incoming calls

Modem

Chassis wiring hub

Some hubs are cabinets with a fixed number of connections. Chassis wiring hubs have expansion slots for a variety of connections. We only recommend them for LANs with 50 or more nodes.

Enterprise network management console

Enterprise network management systems provide detailed data for planning and budgeting, sound alarms when certain parameters exceed set levels, and help in troubleshooting.

Wiring hubs, routers, servers, special probes, and even UPS devices contribute data to the management console for its consolidated displays and reports. The console controls the operation of these devices.

UPS

Central database server

A central client/server database system accepts requests from client PCs, indexes and sorts data tables, and provides complete replies.

We recommend database servers for ordering, inventory, and other major corporate database tasks.

Central backup and hierarchical storage management

Enterprise backup handles critical files on any server regardless of operating system. Hierarchical storage management systems move files to different backup media (such as hard drive, DAT, and optical) as they age.

20 Remote LAN Access

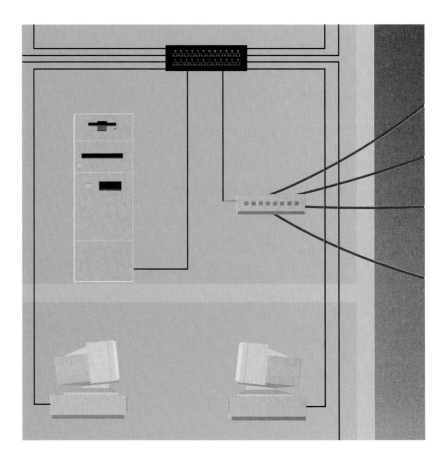

MANY companies have found that there are several reasons to connect a LAN in one office to a LAN in another. For example, LAN-based e-mail only works efficiently if everyone in the organization has access to the e-mail system. Workers in smaller offices often feel "cut off" from the main office when their computers can't communicate.

Remote LAN access provides a simple, effective way to connect one or more remote offices to a central site. Once connected, PCs in the branch offices can use shared resources—like e-mail files, printers, and application servers—on the main office LAN just as if they were sitting at a desk in the main office. Until recently, most remote access products used modem or leased-line links to connect the branch offices. Modems are really too slow for this application, and leased lines are expensive and inflexible.

A new breed of remote access products uses an *ISDN* (Integrated Services Digital Network) line in place of a more expensive (and less flexible) dedicated point-to-point leased line. ISDN provides a fast, flexible, on-demand link between two points. You can use ISDN to connect multiple LANs together on an as-needed basis, or you can connect smaller branch office LANs and even single-workstation "work at home" users. Using ISDN allows a single client PC to connect to more than one host LAN, providing additional flexibility.

Regardless of the type of communications link used, remote LAN products consist of a host unit—called a *router*—and one or more client routers. The host-side router connects to the main-office LAN and to one or more phone lines. The client-side routers are modem-sized boxes that have a communication line interface and a network connector.

The client router automatically dials up the main office when it detects outbound LAN traffic. When LAN traffic drops to zero for a predetermined period of time, the routers disconnect the line. Remote access routers don't require any additional software at either end of the connection, and they don't make any resource demands on the host LAN, the file server, or the client PC.

The remote PC needs a NIC (Network Interface Card) and the appropriate LAN driver software, just as it would if it were connected directly to the main office LAN. Once installed, remote LAN access provides a nearly seamless link between the remote PC and the host LAN.

One of the benefits of ISDN is that it provides two communications channels on each line, and either channel can be used for voice or data traffic. Most client routers have an analog voice port, allowing you to use the ISDN line for voice calls. This is an important feature, since it allows you to maximize your use of the ISDN phone line.

Remote LAN Access

ISDN remote access routers allow several small offices or work-at-home users to connect to the main office LAN at once. You can think of these products as an Ethernet extension cord. Remote users see all shared resources on the main LAN just as they would if they were sitting at a PC in the office. ISDN provides a 128Kbps connection, and data compression can boost that speed to over 500Kbps. Most routers allow use of the ISDN line for voice and fax traffic, eliminating the need for a separate voice or fax line at the remote sites.

A router at the main office connects to the LAN and to one or more communications lines. In this example, the router is connected to a single ISDN line, but most support from 4 to 96 ISDN connections at once. The router watches all the traffic on the LAN. When the router sees data destined for a remote computer, it sends the data over the communications link. After a period of inactivity, the router disconnects the line to save connection charges and to accommodate other inbound calls. The same router that handles remote access can also be used to provide a connection to the Internet via an ISDN or fractional T1 line.

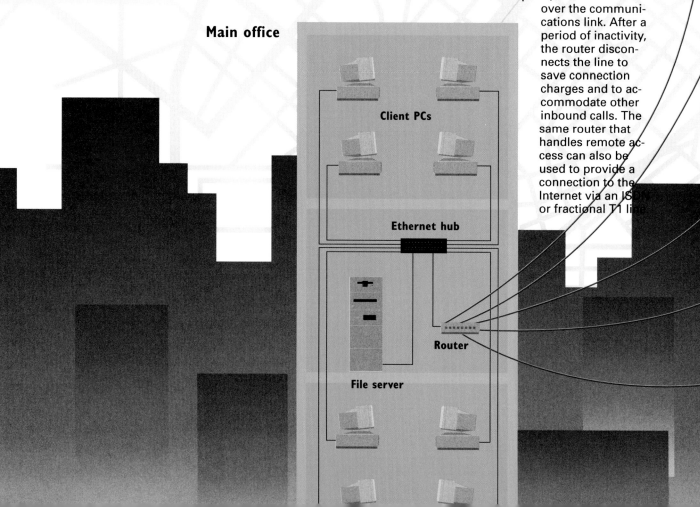

Main office

Client PCs

Ethernet hub

File server

Router

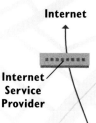

Internet

Internet
Service
Provider

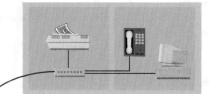

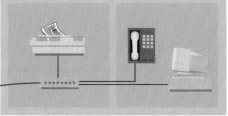

ISDN line

ISDN line

At the remote site, a smaller router connects to the computer and to an ISDN line. Like the main office router, the remote router detects LAN traffic destined for the main office and automatically connects to the main office LAN as necessary. Most ISDN routers provide a telephone and/or fax interface jack, which allows users to make voice and fax calls on the same ISDN line.

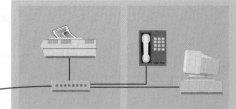

ISDN line

Fax **Telephone**

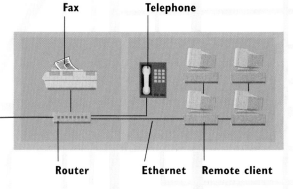

Router **Ethernet** **Remote client**

Fractional T-1 line

Home/remote offices

Larger remote offices may have more WAN traffic than a single ISDN line can handle. Fractional T1 lines provide connection speeds ranging from 128Kbps up to 1.5Mbps. Like ISDN lines, fractional T1 lines can carry voice and data.

CHAPTER
21

Network Security

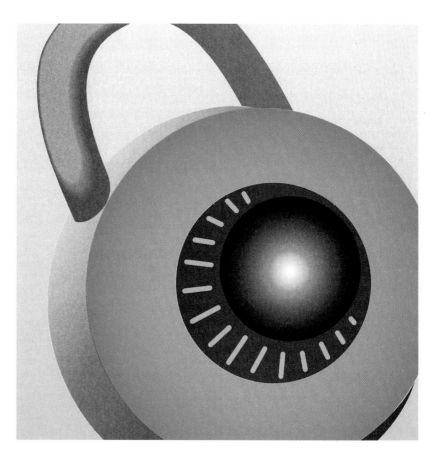

THE data on a corporate network is valuable stuff. Loss or damage to corporate data can be costly. Modern security practices weave layers of physical, administrative, electronic, and encrypted security around valuable data.

In the early days of computing, data security wasn't a major concern. Mainframe computer systems required a closed, air-conditioned environment, and they generally weren't connected to the outside world. To steal data from a mainframe computer, you'd need physical access to the computer itself.

Physical security remains an important factor, but it's even more difficult to enforce with small personal computers. The central computer room, or server room, is making a comeback. Server rooms provide cooling, stable electrical power, and security. They make sense in modern network installations.

During the 1980s, several trends combined to make data security a major concern. First, computers became the hub of most modern businesses. They became the storehouse for inventory, payroll, employee information, design, and manufacturing documents, and, as such, a juicy target. Second, the trend towards networking and open communications led computer makers to adopt common standards for data communication and storage. It became easy to view a file created on an IBM mainframe on a PC. Finally, most large computers became connected to some kind of networking system, either by LAN or modem. Sensitive corporate data came within the reach of anyone clever enough to get it.

In the 1980s, a new type of criminal—the hacker—emerged. Originally used to describe anyone who worked with computers, the term is now almost exclusively applied to people who break into computers. Many hackers do it for profit or for hire as a form of corporate or international espionage. But many others break into computer systems purely for the challenge.

Many older mainframe computers were designed with few security measures beyond password protection. In some cases, all computers with the same operating system shipped with the same maintenance password. If an administrator didn't change the maintenance password, a savvy hacker had an unobstructed ride into the system.

Password protection can be enough security for most systems—provided that people give their passwords the proper handling and respect. An administrative security program focuses on passwords, access rights, and personnel issues. Administrators have to work with managers to ensure that only people with a current need to access information are on authorization lists. Administrators have to teach people that writing their computer passwords down on a desk calendar or on a note taped to their monitors is not a good security practice! The fact is that most intrusions into computer systems involve a compromised password. Passwords should be more than five characters long, random, frequently changed, and protected in order to provide effective security. The most sophisticated electronic security systems are useless without good administrative security practices.

Electronic security techniques are designed to keep hackers away from important data. These techniques operate at different levels, but generally they recognize and accredit the source of the data. Starting with connections from outside the LAN, many modems can receive a call and, on command, dial back the caller at a pre-stored number to foil a would-be intruder. Modems can also use Incoming Caller ID, an optional telephone company feature, to identify calls as coming from an authorized telephone number. Similarly, network operating systems can recognize the embedded addresses of network adapters and associate certain maximum priviliges with specific adapters.

In wide area networks, particularly those with Internet connections, specialized routers, called *firewalls*, carefully inspect each incoming packet looking for authorized source addresses and rejecting any unknown addresses or even suspicious packets. A skillful and determined hacker can generate packets with some correct authorized source information, so sometimes illegal packets are only detected by their process and intent.

Encryption is the final layer of protection. Interestingly, some data compression techniques, used during data transmission and during file storage, act as a primitive form of encryption. It takes a lot more effort to hijack compressed data. Beyond compression, serious encryption systems obscure even the volume of information being transmitted and stored. Some operating systems and electronic mail systems encrypt files during storage, and all commercial-quality network operating systems offer encryption of passwords. Several companies offer encryption modules for routers so that all of the data passing between networked sites is, in practical terms, totally private.

The threat to data exists even in small companies. The larger the monetary stakes, the higher the threat. Good administrative security practices are a must for every organization. You can and should scale electronic protection schemes to match the value of the information and the threat.

Secure Enterprise Networking

Computer network security consists of physical security, administrative security (including proper handling of passwords), and electronic security. Electronic security includes the careful inspection of incoming packets and limitations on authorized telephone connections.

Physical security

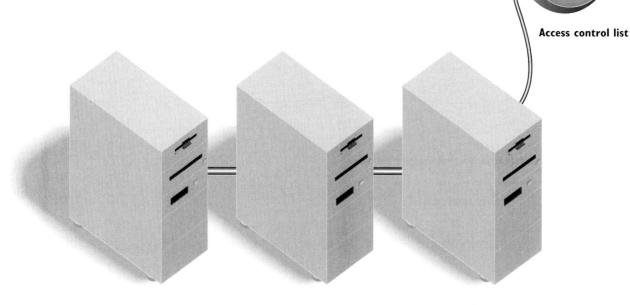

Access control list

Consolidated server room

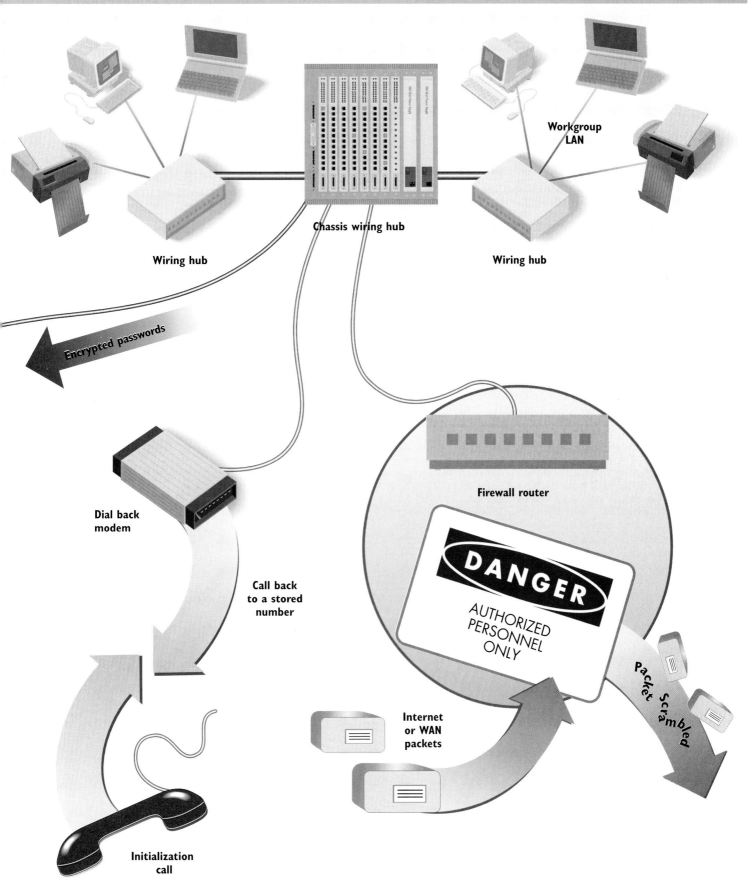

Workgroup
LAN

Chassis wiring hub

Wiring hub

Wiring hub

Encrypted passwords

Firewall router

Dial back
modem

Call back
to a stored
number

DANGER

AUTHORIZED
PERSONNEL
ONLY

Packet Scrambled

Internet
or WAN
packets

Initialization
call

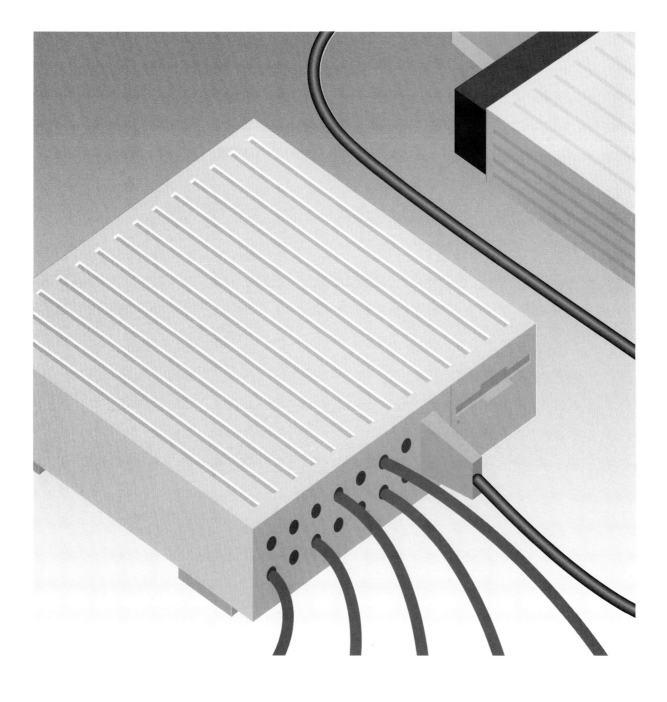

P A R T

LINKS BETWEEN LANS

INFORMATION is the raw material, inventory, and processed product of many modern organizations.

Computer networks are the production line, distribution system, and even the retail point of sale for the information products generated by many organizations and businesses. These networks act as local, regional, and international distribution systems for modern commerce.

If local area networks (LANs) are like the in-house production lines of manufacturing plants, then computer networks that cover the distances between cities and countries are the roads and rail lines of modern businesses. Long-distance data networks, called *metropolitan area networks* (*MANs*), and *wide area networks* (*WANs*) are the equivalent of the trucking, rail, barge, and air freight systems needed to support smokestack industries.

Because many organizations need to move a lot of data over distances greater than a few thousand feet, the industry developed several techniques for extending and linking LANs. The techniques you select to link LAN segments depend on the distance and speed needed, the network communications protocols in use, and your business's philosophy regarding leasing versus owning facilities.

Just as some manufacturing companies own their own trucks and boxcars, and others contract for all transportation services, some organizations own their MAN and WAN facilities, and others lease these specialized services from commercial suppliers. Many organizations set up their own microwave, light beam, or fiber optic transmission systems to carry data around a metropolitan area or campus. Organizations can use the transportation tunnels under many cities to install their own fiber optic cable systems between their offices or stores and major customers and suppliers. Metropolitan telephone and cable television companies also supply LAN-to-LAN connections under several types of business arrangements. But when the connections extend beyond the metropolitan area, organizations typically lease circuits from suppliers such as the long-haul telephone carriers AT&T and MCI, specialized companies such as Tymnet and Telenet, and satellite system providers such as GTE.

When you lease circuits for links between LANs, you have many options. The three general technical categories of leased services are *circuit-switched, full-period*, and *packet-switched*. Circuit-switched services are those with a dial tone; for example, switched-56 digital services and the Integrated Services Digital Network (ISDN). The equipment dials a connection, transfers data, and hangs up when it completes the transaction. Full-period services, such as leased telephone lines, provide a circuit dedicated to your use full time.

Packet-switched systems allow multipoint connections for bursts of short packets. Packet-switched networks are also called X.25 networks after an older CCITT packet-switching standard; today, these networks commonly use a newer standard called *frame relay*.

To lease a circuit to link LAN segments will cost, typically, thousands of dollars a month. The cost is determined by the maximum signaling speed desired and sometimes by the distance. Therefore, it makes sense to invest in network portal devices for both ends of the link that can use the expensive circuit to maximum efficiency.

Network traffic typically follows specific paths and travels within a group of people with common business interests—a workgroup. However, some traffic also flows between workgroups. Putting all workgroups on the same cable and letting them communicate without restrictions consumes the available resources of the cable. Organizations with busy networks can use network portal devices called bridges that link workgroup LANs while exercising discrimination over the traffic passing between them.

A router is a more complex portal device than a bridge and has a greater ability to examine and direct the traffic it carries. Routers are somewhat more expensive to buy and require more attention than bridges, but their more robust features make them the best choice for a portal between a LAN and a long-distance link.

A router reads the destination address of the network packet and determines if it is on the same segment of network cable as the originating station. If the destination station is on the other side of the bridge, the bridge sequences the packet into the traffic on that cable segment.

Routers read the more complex network addressing information in the packet or token and may add more information to get the packet through the network. For example, a router might wrap an Ethernet packet in an "envelope" of data containing routing and transmission information for transmission through an X.25 packet-switched network. When the envelope of data comes out the other end of the X.25 network, the receiving router strips off the X.25 data, readdresses the Ethernet packet, and sequences it on its attached LAN segment.

Routers make very smart connections between the elements of complex networks. Routers can choose from redundant paths between LAN segments, and they can link LAN segments using very different data packaging and media access schemes.

A new technology, Asynchronous Transfer Mode (ATM), is becoming more important as network traffic includes more time-sensitive video and digitized sound data.

CHAPTER
22

Repeaters, Bridges, Routers, and Switches

JUST as manufacturing plants have mail rooms and shipping docks, local area networks have specified places—called *portals*—where the local and long-distance services meet. Portal devices—repeaters, bridges, and routers—extend and segment the local area network's high-speed cable, and each device offers a different degree of discrimination and data handling capability.

A *repeater*, typically a little box you can hold in your hand, connects two segments of your network cable; the repeater retimes and regenerates the digital signals on the cable and sends them on their way again. Bridges and routers are more complex and expensive devices that can be found within personal computers, as stand-alone devices on the LAN, and as modules that are part of wiring hubs. *Bridges* read the station address of each Ethernet packet or of a Token-Ring frame—the outermost envelope around the data—to determine the destination of the message, but they do not look inside the packet or frame to read NetBIOS, IPX, or TCP/IP addresses. A *router* digs deeper into the envelopes surrounding the data to find the destination for the data packet. A *router* reads the information contained in each packet or frame, uses complex network addressing procedures to determine the appropriate network destination, discards the outer packet or frame, and then repackages and retransmits the data using compression. When routers connect LANs, it doesn't matter what kinds of hardware the LAN segments use and, because multiprotocol routers are available, the LAN segments don't even have to use the same network communications protocols. Because they don't pass, or even handle, every packet or frame, routers act as a safety barrier between network segments. Data packets with errors simply don't make it through the router.

Routers strip off the outer layers of Ethernet or Token-Ring data before they send a packet from one LAN to the other, so they reduce the total number of bits going across the inter-LAN communications link. The remote router at the receiving end repackages the data into a packet or frame appropriate for its LAN segment. This allows routers to send the information across the inter-LAN circuit more efficiently than bridges do, and you can use less costly long-distance circuits.

If the two networks use the same network signaling and access-control protocol, such as Ethernet, the networks can be linked with a bridge on each LAN. But if the networks are different—for example, if one uses Ethernet and the other uses Token-Ring—routers would be the best choice.

A new inter-LAN technology called Asynchronous Transfer Mode (ATM) switching takes all types of data, including LAN traffic, video, and digitized sound, and packages it into small 54-byte segments called *cells*. The small cell size reduces the delay any one cell can experience if it is delayed by the passage of any other cell. So, sound and movement stay synchronized. Because ATM switches move cells along one path toward their destination, ATM systems do not need bridges or routers. ATM switches are discussed in Chapter 25.

Repeaters, Bridges, and Routers

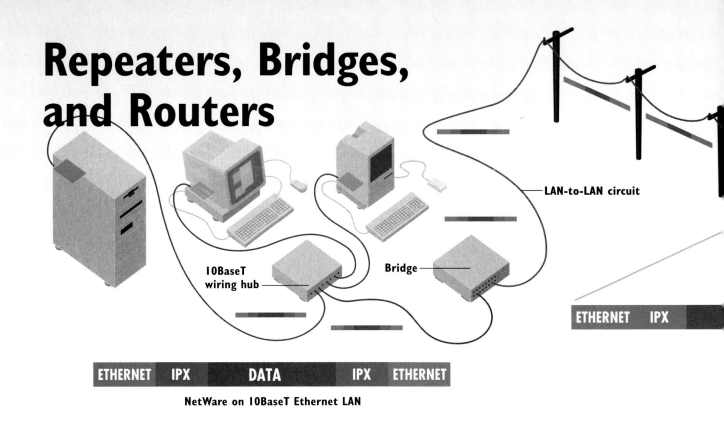

ETHERNET   IPX   DATA   IPX   ETHERNET

NetWare on 10BaseT Ethernet LAN

The routers examine the destination address contained in the NetWare IPX protocol. They strip off the Ethernet packet or Token-Ring frame information and send only the IPX packet and its encapsulated data across the inter-LAN link. This action significantly reduces the amount of data on the inter-LAN circuit—reducing circuit costs—and provides a way to link networks that use very different networking schemes, such as Ethernet and Token-Ring. Both LANs in this example use NetWare's IPX, but sophisticated multiprotocol routers are also available.

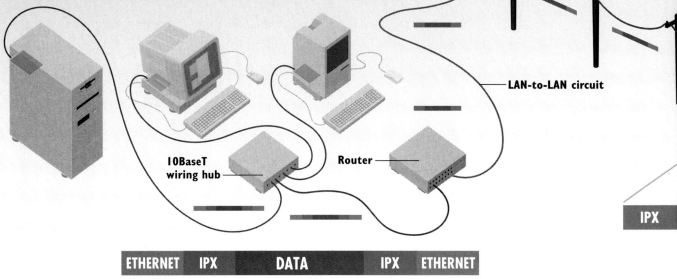

ETHERNET   IPX   DATA   IPX   ETHERNET

NetWare on 10BaseT Ethernet LAN

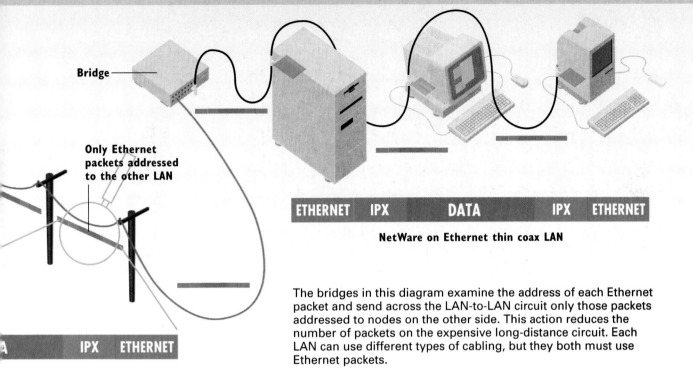

Only Ethernet packets addressed to the other LAN

ETHERNET	IPX	DATA	IPX	ETHERNET

NetWare on Ethernet thin coax LAN

A	IPX	ETHERNET

The bridges in this diagram examine the address of each Ethernet packet and send across the LAN-to-LAN circuit only those packets addressed to nodes on the other side. This action reduces the number of packets on the expensive long-distance circuit. Each LAN can use different types of cabling, but they both must use Ethernet packets.

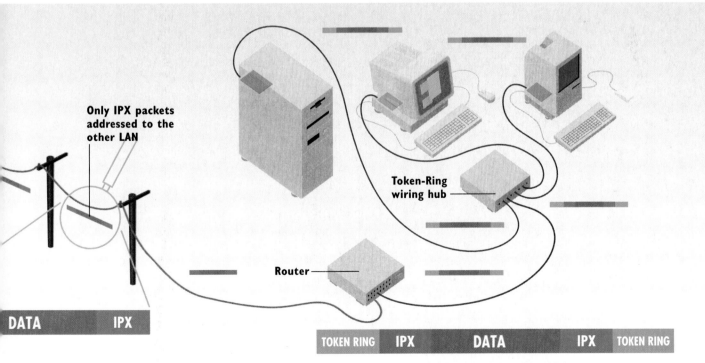

Only IPX packets addressed to the other LAN

Token-Ring wiring hub

Router

DATA	IPX

TOKEN RING	IPX	DATA	IPX	TOKEN RING

NetWare on Token-Ring LAN

CHAPTER
23

Metropolitan Area Networks (MANs)

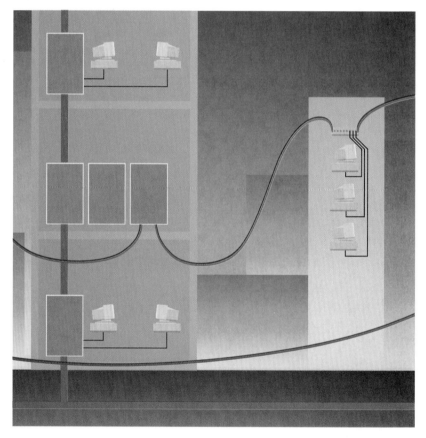

LANs

are, by definition local—within 1000 feet or so. As businesses and other organizations grow, administrators must find a way to link the LANs within a campus or a city. A *Metropolitan Area Network* (*MAN*) presents a unique set of problems and opportunities.

The most common link between networks today is a digital telephone line leased from the local telephone company. But this type of service usually carries signaling speed and mileage charges, and is one of the most expensive links you can buy. There are other, more specialized services designed for data connections.

The IEEE 802.6 committee studies metropolitan area networks. This committee is developing a standard called the *Distributed Queue Dual Bus* (*DQDB*). The DQDB topology includes two parallel runs of cable (typically fiber optic) linking each node (typically a router for a LAN segment) on the system. This dual cable system provides high reliability and signaling rates in the range of 100 megabits per second.

The IEEE 802.6 MAN is designed as a metropolitan utility serving a large number of organizations across an area of many miles. In the United States, IEEE 802.6 MANs probably will be installed and run by the local telephone companies.

Another service, called *Fiber Distributed Data Interface* (*FDDI*), provides a backbone of communications services across town and can act as a traffic-gathering system to feed the DQDB backbone. FDDI systems have a sustained throughput of about 80 megabits per second and are limited to about 60 miles of cable. Companies can economically install FDDI systems for their own use and to sell as a service to anyone in the extended neighborhood. Many companies sell FDDI network adapters, so they can be used as a local network connection alternative within a building and then extended to the metropolitan environment.

The FDDI architecture uses two rings of fiber to carry data. All nodes attach to the primary ring, but since the secondary ring is designed to provide a backup connection, some nodes (called *Class B stations*) might not attach to the secondary ring for reasons of economy.

Finally, you can make wireless inter-LAN connections within a metropolitan area, particularly if you have at least one office with a top-down view of the skyline. Several companies—including M/A-Com, MicroWave Networks, Inc., and Motorola Microwave—sell microwave radios operating at 23 gigahertz (GHz) that can be, literally, pointed out the window toward the distant LAN. Microwave is a reasonably economical option for distances of up to 20 miles: It offers signaling speeds of 1.544 megabits per second and, at a typical cost of $10,000 to $15,000 per set, there are no monthly leased-line charges.

You would usually lease metropolitan area LAN-to-LAN circuits from your telephone company and from other vendors. But installing your own links is an excellent alternative for many organizations.

Metropolitan Area Networks

The organization in this well-connected office building extends its local area network using digital circuits leased from the local telephone company, microwave radio connections to a nearby operating location, and an FDDI network to three LANs in the metropolitan area.

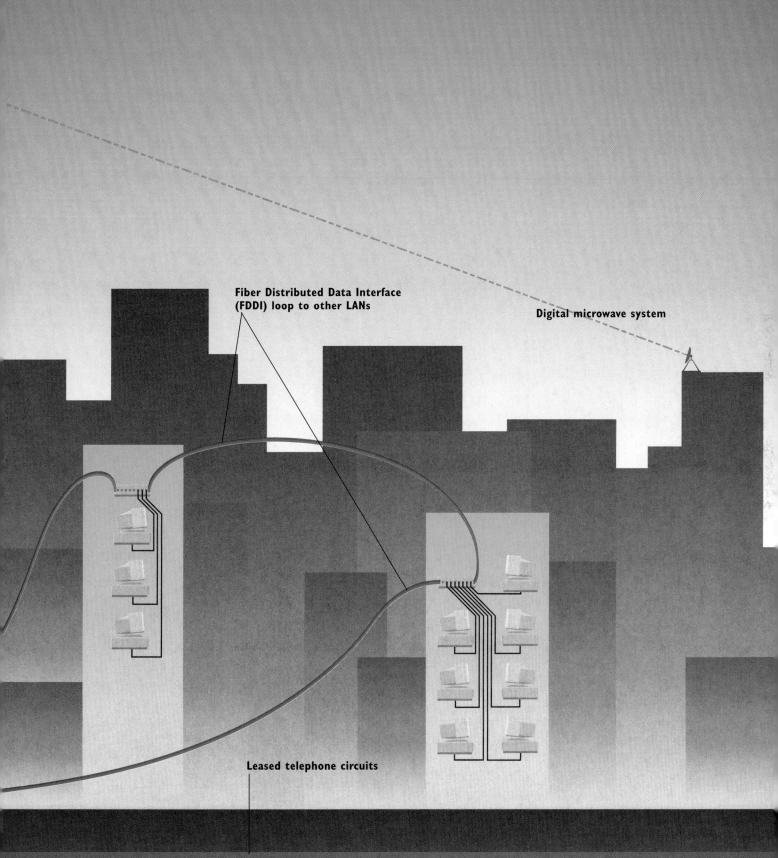

Fiber Distributed Data Interface
(FDDI) loop to other LANs

Digital microwave system

Leased telephone circuits

C H A P T E R
24

Circuit-Switched Digital Services

THE laws of physics dictate that a signal degrades as it passes over a cable. Network engineers have to employ expensive equipment and techniques to preserve data integrity and move that data quickly over long distances. The formula is *speed × distance = cost.*

Instead of paying for LAN-to-LAN links on a full-time basis, you can dial up digital connections as you need them. Circuits that you dial up to make a connection are called *circuit-switched digital services.* Generally, a circuit-switched digital service is more economical than a leased line service if you need connections for only three to eight hours a day, or less. Circuit-switched digital services are perfect for linking electronic-mail servers on different LANs and for doing tasks such as updating inventory and order records from one network database to another at the end of each day.

The major portions of the public telephone systems are fully digital. They handle voice and data as a stream of 0's and 1's instead of analog tones. Only the last few miles of cable carry data in analog form. The only difference between the circuit-switched voice connection of phone calls and the circuit-switched data connections occurs in the cable between the telephone company's central office and the termination. Voice circuits use an older type of wiring system meant to eliminate distortion of the voice. Modems for voice circuits convert data to tones that traverse a few miles of cable until they become data again at the central office. When telephone companies install switched digital services, new wiring systems carry the data in digital form all the way and there is no need for modems.

Circuit-switched service vendors offer dial-up circuits able to carry maximum signaling rates of 56, 64, and 384 kilobits per second and 1.544 megabits per second. Switched data circuits follow the same pricing scheme as switched voice circuits. You pay for equipment and installation, a monthly service charge, and for each call by the minute according to the distance. In some areas, switched-56 service costs no more than voice service.

The Integrated Services Digital Network (ISDN) is a circuit-switched digital service. ISDN marketing literature stresses combined voice and data applications, but companies such as Digiboard and Microcom market practical ISDN routers for LAN-to-LAN services. These devices establish an ISDN circuit-switched digital connection between appropriate LANs when traffic appears, and then break down the connection when it is no longer needed.

The most popular ISDN service for linking LANs is *basic rate interface,* or BRI. This service delivers two data channels able to carry 64 kilobits per second each, called bearer channels, or *B channels,* and a separate 16-kilobit-per-second channel, called the data channel, or *D channel.* The D channel is used to signal the computers in the telephone switching system to generate calls, reset calls, and receive information about incoming calls, including the identity of the caller.

Circuit-switched digital services can provide handy and economical connections between LANs. They are a useful alternative to metropolitan and long-distance inter-LAN connections.

Circuit-Switched Digital Network

The central office of every local telephone company is a computerized switch that works with other similar switches to route and complete a call—that's where the term *circuit switching* comes from.

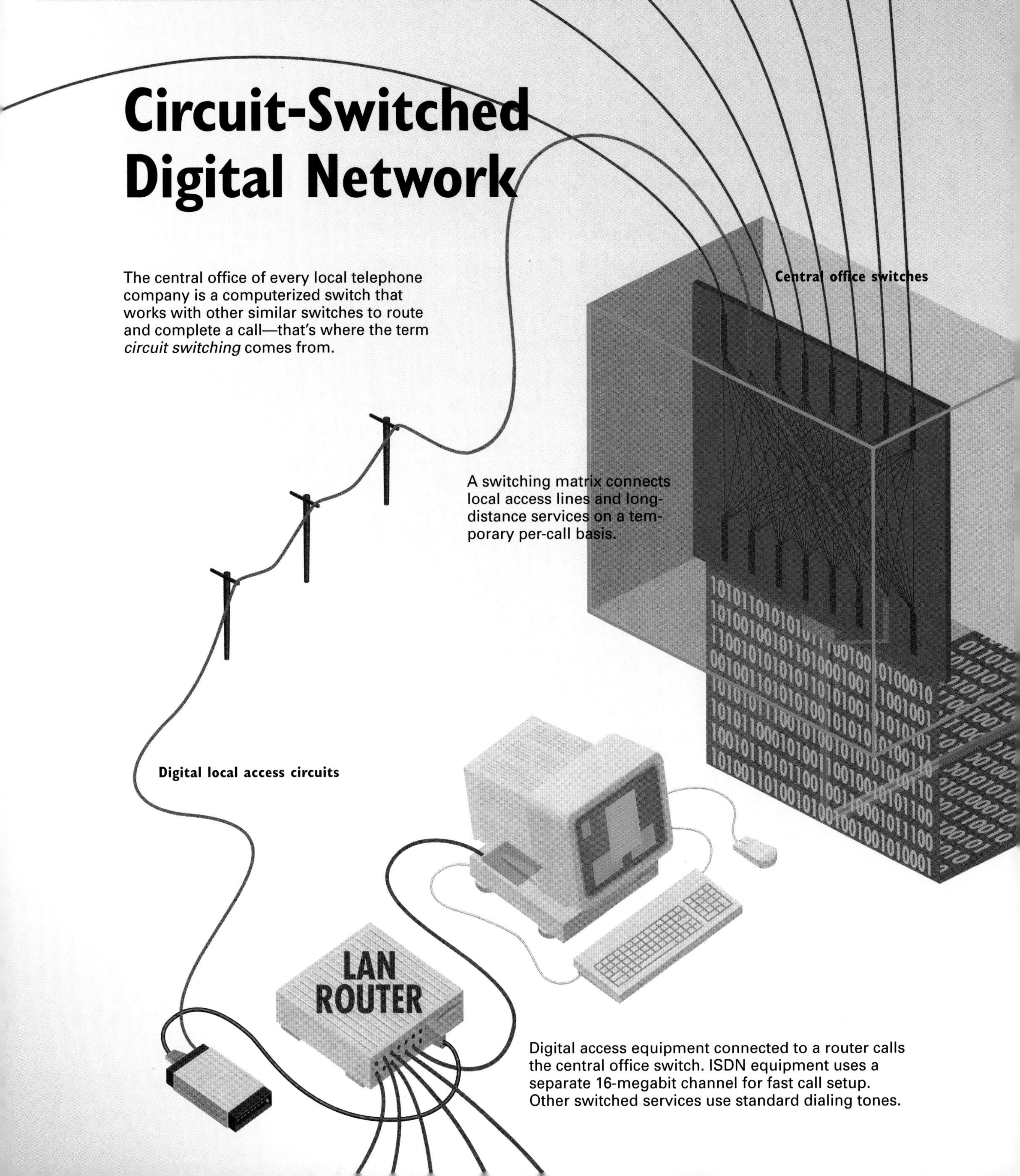

Central office switches

A switching matrix connects local access lines and long-distance services on a temporary per-call basis.

Digital local access circuits

Digital access equipment connected to a router calls the central office switch. ISDN equipment uses a separate 16-megabit channel for fast call setup. Other switched services use standard dialing tones.

LAN ROUTER

A high-speed intraswitch trunk is
often a fiber optic link operating at
45 megabits.

Digital local access circuits

LAN
ROUTER

ISDN—Painless Voice and Data

There are two types of ISDN lines. Because phone company people invented these names, they're long and technical. Don't let this put you off.

The Internet

Router

Basic Rate Interface (BRI) lines provide two data channels, called bearer channels, or B channels. Each B channel can carry voice or data at 64 kilobits per second—better than twice the speed of a V.34 modem. Each B channel operates independently of the other, and each can have its own phone number. Your computer can use one B channel for data while you're talking on the other.

Primary Rate Interface (PRI) lines provide 23 B channels and are typically used for large installations that require many lines.

All ISDN lines also have a single data channel, or D channel. The D channel carries information between your ISDN equipment and the telephone company's central office. BRI lines are sometimes called 2B+D lines; PRI lines are called 23B+D lines.

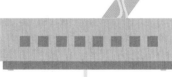

Router

PC

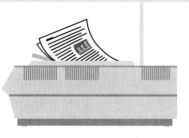

Network printer

Server

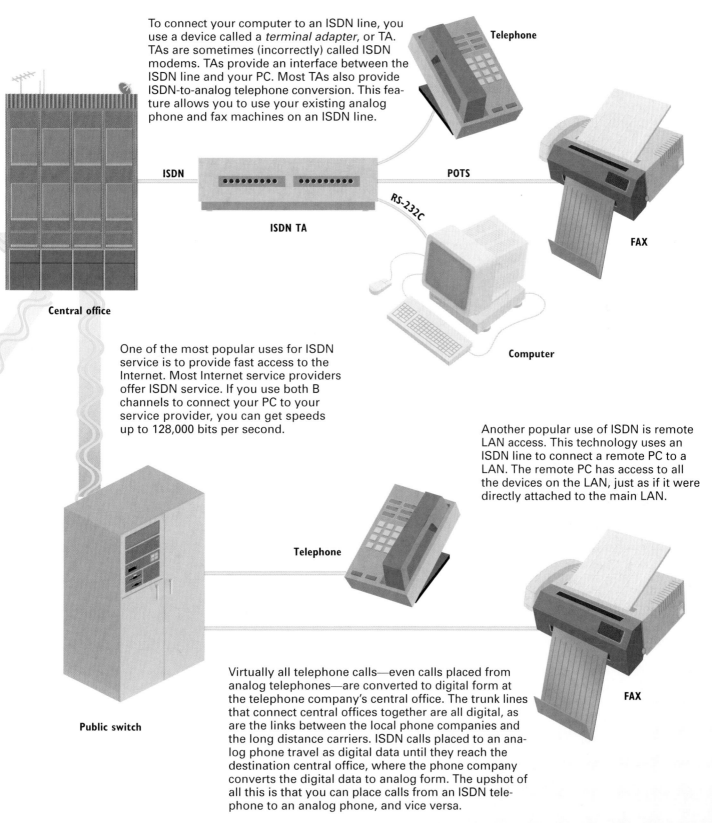

To connect your computer to an ISDN line, you use a device called a *terminal adapter*, or TA. TAs are sometimes (incorrectly) called ISDN modems. TAs provide an interface between the ISDN line and your PC. Most TAs also provide ISDN-to-analog telephone conversion. This feature allows you to use your existing analog phone and fax machines on an ISDN line.

Telephone

ISDN

POTS

RS-232C

ISDN TA

FAX

Central office

Computer

One of the most popular uses for ISDN service is to provide fast access to the Internet. Most Internet service providers offer ISDN service. If you use both B channels to connect your PC to your service provider, you can get speeds up to 128,000 bits per second.

Another popular use of ISDN is remote LAN access. This technology uses an ISDN line to connect a remote PC to a LAN. The remote PC has access to all the devices on the LAN, just as if it were directly attached to the main LAN.

Telephone

Virtually all telephone calls—even calls placed from analog telephones—are converted to digital form at the telephone company's central office. The trunk lines that connect central offices together are all digital, as are the links between the local phone companies and the long distance carriers. ISDN calls placed to an analog phone travel as digital data until they reach the destination central office, where the phone company converts the digital data to analog form. The upshot of all this is that you can place calls from an ISDN telephone to an analog phone, and vice versa.

FAX

Public switch

C H A P T E R
25

Packet-Switching Networks

ANOTHER technological alternative for LAN-to-LAN connections is packet-switching networks. This category includes X.25, frame-relay, and cell-relay technologies. Packet switching has been more popular in Europe and Asia than in the United States because many U.S. organizations depend on leased-line services. However, aggressive pricing of frame relay is making it popular in North America.

The major appeal of packet-switching services comes from their flexible multipoint capabilities. LANs in many different locations can exchange data with one central location and with each other. The LAN portals can use different signaling rates and the packet-switched network buffers the data. Commercial packet-switching networks are also called *public-data networks* (*PDNs*)—or *value-added networks* (*VANs*)—because of the error-control, buffering, and protocol conversion they can provide.

Although the other LAN-to-LAN alternatives typically involve flat monthly fees, determined by distance and speed, packet-switching networks are, in a term of the trade, *usage sensitive*. That is, you pay a basic monthly service charge and a fee based on the amount of data received by each of your ports on the network. Usage-sensitive billing can make packet-switching networks more attractive than full-period leased lines when your applications transfer data only a few times a day.

Full-period connections to the packet-switched network are available from your network portal device, and usually operate at rates of 56 kilobits through 1.544 megabits per second. The carrier you choose can make all the arrangements for the service and present the charges in one bill.

Until 1991, a protocol called X.25 dominated packet-switched networks. This protocol uses a belt-and-suspenders design to ensure the delivery and integrity of data shipped across the network. But networks using reliable digital circuits don't need all the accounting and checking provided by the X.25 protocol, so designers stripped off many X.25 functions, reduced the overhead, and developed a service called *frame relay*. Several standards organizations adopted important frame-relay standards in 1991 and some vendors first offered frame-relay service intermixed with X.25. Today the focus of most service providers is on frame relay.

New developments in packet-switched systems center on cell-switching technologies. Because the X.25 packet and the frame-relay frame are of variable length, the network must constantly adjust the flow and timing of messages. If the data bundles are all the same size, the network designers can tighten up the operation, gaining efficiency and reducing the complexity of the system. A technology generally called *cell relay* and an evolving cell-relay standard called *asynchronous transfer mode* (ATM) are designed for very heavy data loads. Operating at speeds of 1.544 megabits per second to 1.2 gigabits per second, ATM cells consist of 48 bytes of application information plus 5 bytes for the header. Network equipment can quickly route and move these uniformly sized bundles of data.

ATM is optimal for carrying digitized voice and video signals because the small cells offer little delay (a feature called *low latency*) as they transit the network. ATM is primarily a wide area network backbone technology.

Packet-switched systems offer reliability and flexibility for LAN-to-LAN connections. There is little up-front cost, and you can have service where you need it, when you need it, and for only as long as you need it.

Packet-Switching Network

LAN
ROUTER

X.25 OR FRAME
RELAY INTERFACE

Digital access lines. Typical
rates are 19.2Kb to 1.544Mb
per second.

Functions of a packet switch:
- Check valid packet
- Check destination address
- Monitor traffic on links
- Check trouble reports
- Determine best route
- Put packets in order
- Retransmit on request
- Initiate error recovery

Packet switch

Packet switch

Intraswitch trunks provide alternative paths to ensure network reliability.

Each packet contains addressing, routing, timing, checksum, and other network information. Frame-relay packets contain less recovery information. If a frame-relay packet is lost or damaged, higher-level programs retransmit the data.

Packet switch

Digital access lines

X.25 OR FRAME RELAY INTERFACE

LAN ROUTER

How an ATM Switch Works

The ATM switch takes a variety of inputs, including LAN data, formats them into small cells, and then routes the cells to other switches on the route.

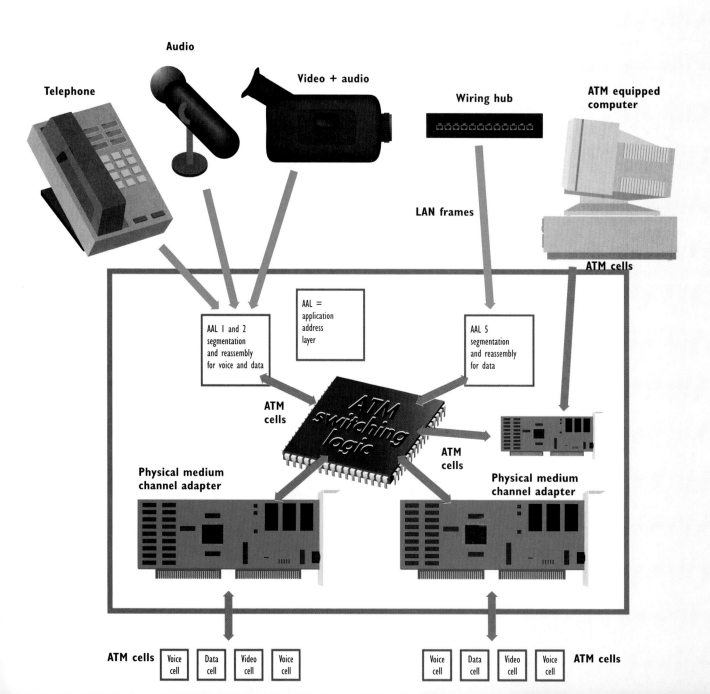

How ATM Changes Packets into Cells

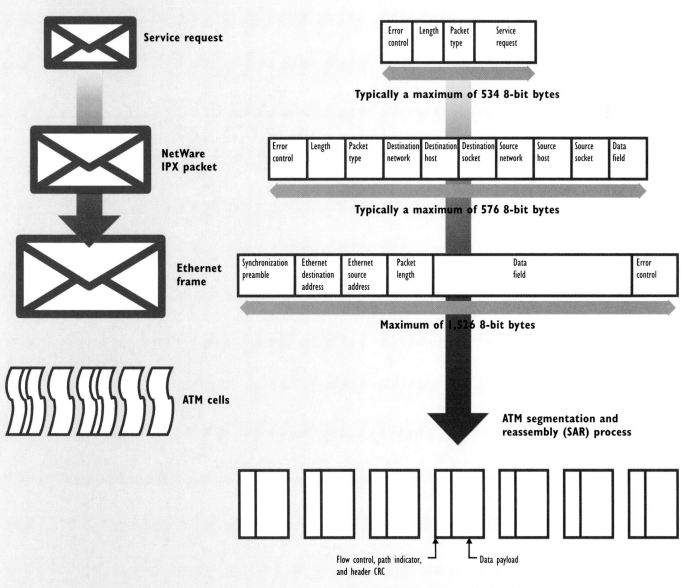

Service request

Error control	Length	Packet type	Service request

Typically a maximum of 534 8-bit bytes

NetWare
IPX packet

Error control	Length	Packet type	Destination network	Destination host	Destination socket	Source network	Source host	Source socket	Data field

Typically a maximum of 576 8-bit bytes

Ethernet frame

Synchronization preamble	Ethernet destination address	Ethernet source address	Packet length	Data field	Error control

Maximum of 1,526 8-bit bytes

ATM cells

ATM segmentation and reassembly (SAR) process

Flow control, path indicator, and header CRC ⌐   ⌐ Data payload

Each ATM cell is always 54 8-bit bytes

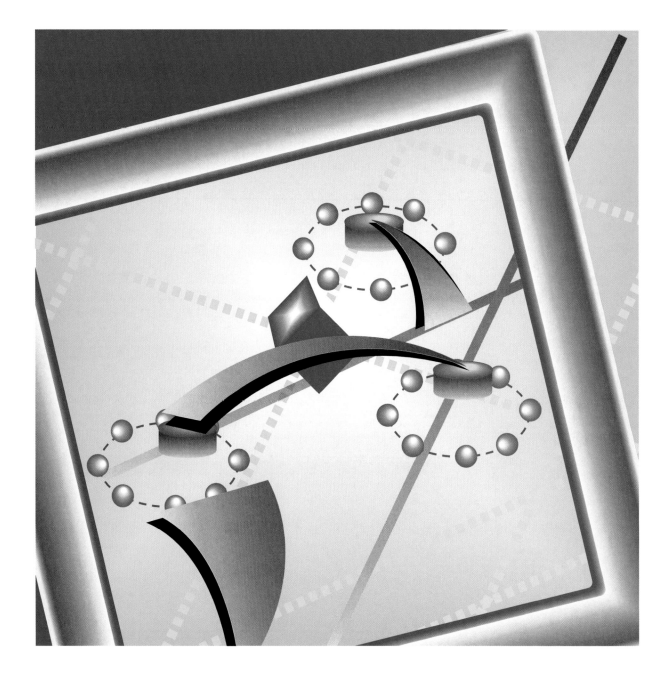

P A R T

5

The Internet

As big as the Internet is, it is only the most visible manifestation of the worldwide adoption of a standard. As explosive as the growth of the Internet seems to be, it didn't happen overnight. As free and as easy as it seems to be, the Internet came from an authoritarian background. Today's Internet traces its roots directly to work sponsored by the U.S. Department of Defense. The DoD needed a communications architecture for its command and control systems that was self-healing, reliable, and universal. The requirement was for computers of different makes, models, and operating systems to communicate across a network with a wide range of delay, throughput, and packet loss. In the late 1960s, the Defense Advanced Research Projects Agency, working with industry and universities, started a network that was simultaneously a tool and a test. This network, the ARPANET, was the development ground for the protocols and techniques used to communicate across today's Internet.

In the 1980s the DoD's Defense Communications Agency acted as the guardian of the standards, but in the 1990s the roles of developer, engineer, and guardian for the emerging Internet passed to the Internet Architecture Board (IAB), an independent organization. The IAB has two principal subsidiary working groups, the Internet Engineering Task Force (IETF) and the Internet Research Task Force (IRTF). If you follow the computer and communications news, you'll often hear about the IAB and the IETF as they try to optimize the Internet for its role in modern business and culture.

The IAB maintains a large library of documents online and it would be impossible to write a book of this type without frequent reference to them. Fortunately, it's easy for you to read the same source materials. The IAB uses Requests for Comments (RFCs) and Standards (STD) to describe concepts and standards. The RFCs often contain proposals from different commercial vendors and a few are even intentionally humorous. The STDs contain the coordinated and accepted descriptions of how things should work—the protocols. Try pointing your browser at `http://sunsite.auc.dk/RFC` for a full list of pages and links or, if that link doesn't work for you, search on RFC-2000. This RFC defines the IAB standards process and contains links to other RFCs and STDs and it should lead you to a library.

The RFCs and STDs go beyond basic connectivity and describe the network management, electronic mail, file transfer, and other functions used on the Internet and on other IP networks. The IAB has created and is expanding a complete computing environment based on layered and flexible protocols. In a computer communications system, software and firmware are designed to conform to specific protocols. There is an important point here that's worth stating another way: Software implements protocols, so protocols like TCP/IP are not software. Programmers use protocols and standards to design software. Knowing the relationship between the protocols and the software can avoid confusion in many discussions.

In modern computers, software is modular and functionally appears to be configured in layers. Data passes up and down through the layers and each layer serves to provide a common interface to the layer above while performing tasks that are specific to some processor, operating system, or peripheral device. Driver software, residing on the bottom layer of an operating system such as Windows, passes data to and from (it "drives") devices such as LAN adapters, serial ports, and communications adapters.

The initial layers of software follow the rules of the protocol by packaging the data coming from the application program into packets. Each packet is like a standardized envelope for data, complete with its own addressing and the equivalent of a postal code, street name, and house number. The packet envelope contains specific information such as the identification of the node originating the packet, the packet's size, and its destination address. Because your message is likely to be made up of many packets, and because they can easily get delivered out of order, they also are labeled as the first, second, third, and so on. One of the duties of TCP is to reorder them in your computer before presenting them as a cohesive message to your application program. Both the format of the packet and its introductory information follow specific rules for that protocol. Through the use of a common protocol, computers with completely different operating systems and processor hardware can exchange data that can be used by applications. That ubiquity is the magnetic appeal of the Internet and the World Wide Web. In the following pages we show you how the complex elements of the Internet function to make it seems easy to gather information, exchange mail, and perform other complex functions.

CHAPTER 26

Internet Connections

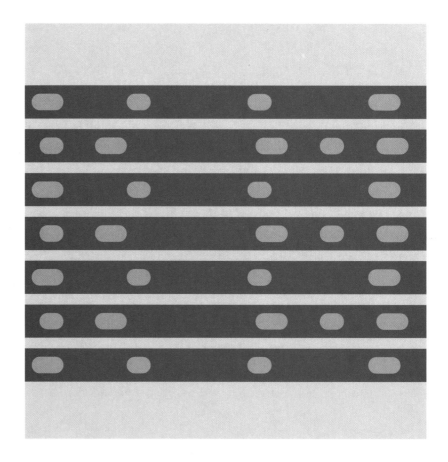

THE Internet is a compound word describing an immense number of agreements, arrangements, and connections. The Internet is literally a network of networks. In fact, it is typically a network of local area networks. A good analogy is between the Internet and a system of bridges linking millions of islands of various sizes. Each island has specific resources and capabilities and each island is its own domain and has a domain name to match. For shipping and delivery purposes, the domain names have affiliated addresses. Similarly, each Internet resource has a domain name and an IP address to match. In our island system, as in the Internet, many different companies built the bridges connecting the island domains and some bridge systems are a little wider or sturdier than others, but together the entire system gives you a world to travel.

Some islands are private. You can establish an *intranet* for your organization that provides Internet-like services, but only for your employees or the members of your group. If you want to extend access to your close business partners, such as suppliers, retailers, or accountants, you can establish a limited-access *extranet*. An intranet or extranet might have only a small bridge to the Internet.

The services of the Internet make it appear as different things to different people. You might think of the World Wide Web portion of the Internet as a place to do research or order products. You're also probably familiar with the electronic mail services of the Internet or your intranet. There are dozens of other services that work over the Internet to provide activities such as keyboard-to-keyboard chatting, real-time voice conversation, and the transfer, storage, and retrieval of files.

Technically, the Internet is an interconnected network based on the TCP/IP family of protocols. *TCP* (the *Transmission Control Protocol*) and *IP* (the *Internet Protocol*) are two protocols, or sets of rules, that govern how computers communicate with one another. A cluster of other affiliated protocols has grown around TCP/IP, and the entire family is regulated and maintained by the Internet Engineering Task Force. Together, they determine how computers connect to one another and how they reliably exchange information. An important part of the IP protocol is the *IP address*. The IP addressing standard—four numbers between 1 and 256 separated by periods— defines a mechanism to provide a unique address for each computer on the Internet.

Additional protocols define activities that two connected computers can perform. For example, the *Post Office Protocol* (*POP*) controls electronic mail and the *Hypertext Transfer Protocol* (*HTTP*) is the basis for the World Wide Web. There are dozens of others, but all Internet protocols work over the TCP/IP protocols.

Today, anyone can subscribe to an Internet Service Provider, or *ISP*. An ISP typically leases a high-speed connection to the Internet backbone network and provides lower-speed access to a number of users. The ISP also provides a variety of value-added services such as e-mail and Web pages with local content. You connect to the ISP via modem, ISDN, or other service such as a cable modem, and the ISP routes your TCP/IP packets to and from the Internet.

The following pages graphically describe the various elements of the large interconnected system called the Internet. We start with the Internet backbone and ISP connections and then show you how the most important protocols work.

How the Internet Connects

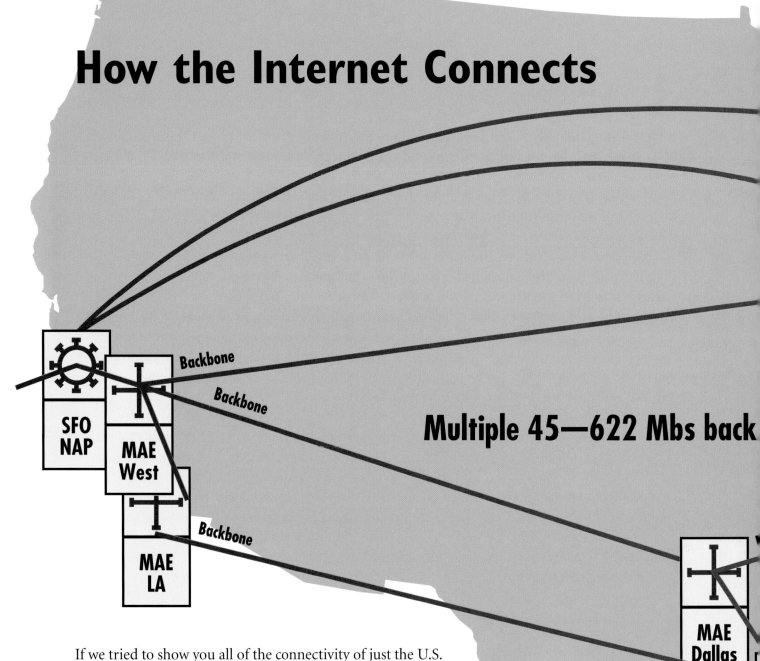

Backbone

Backbone

Multiple 45—622 Mbs back

SFO NAP

MAE West

MAE LA

Backbone

MAE Dallas

If we tried to show you all of the connectivity of just the U.S. Internet, the map would be black with crossing lines. In the U.S., the fundamental Internet connectivity consists of overlapping and interconnecting digital backbone circuits of 45–622Mbs provided by more than two dozen carriers. These circuits meet at the four Network Access Points and several Metropolitan Area Exchanges shown on this map. However, the major carriers and hundreds of other carriers also interconnect at hundreds of other points. The result is immense capacity and the ability to survive catastrophes. The carriers have redundant connections to points around the world. The backbones typically feed multiple 45Mbs links that fan out to metropolitan centers. The backbones continue to expand and increase capacity.

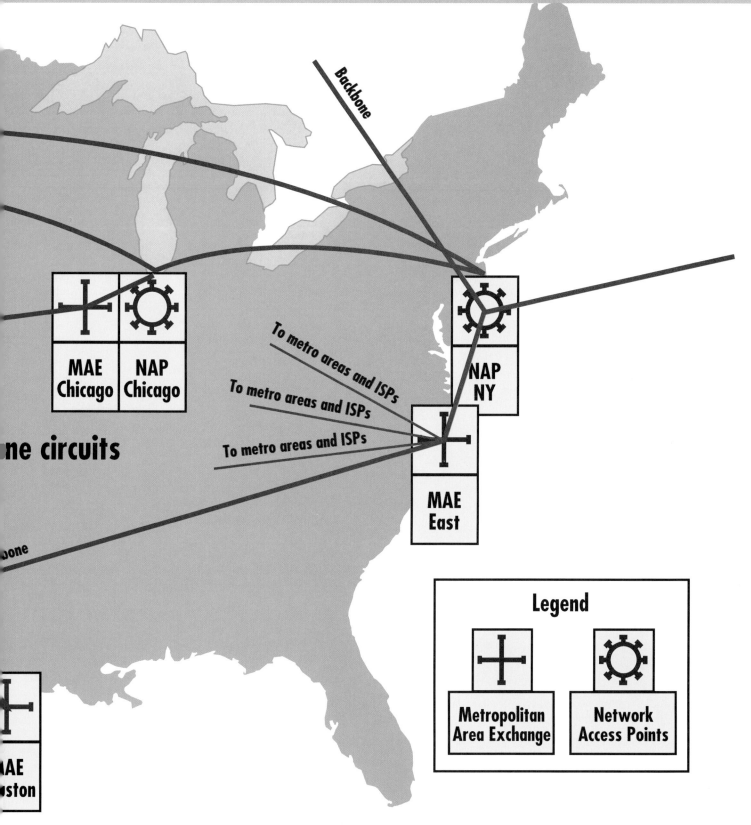

Backbone

To metro areas and ISPs

To metro areas and ISPs

To metro areas and ISPs

To metro areas and ISPs

MAE
Chicago

NAP
Chicago

NAP
NY

MAE
East

ne circuits

oone

AE
ston

Legend

Metropolitan
Area Exchange

Network
Access Points

How Local Access Works

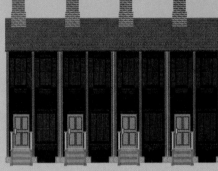

Condos

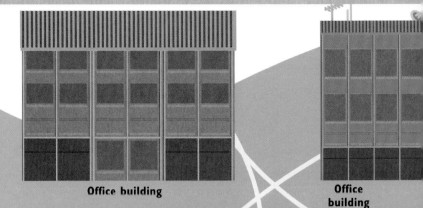

Office building

Office building

Standard telephone lines carry dial-up or ISDN connections from users. The telephone company aggregates the data into a digital line to the ISP.

Competitive local exchange carrier telephone switch

Internet Service Providers (ISPs) use leased digital lines to link to the Internet backbone. They use telephone lines from the local telephone companies and cable television companies to reach end users. ISPs include Internet backbone carriers, telephone companies, and companies specializing in the ISP business. A U.S. metropolitan area might have 300 competing ISPs.

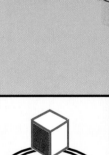

ISP

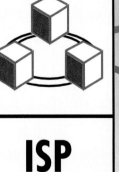

ISP

Links of up to 45Mbs connect ISPs to an Internet backbone carrier site—often an MAE.

Internet backbone connecti

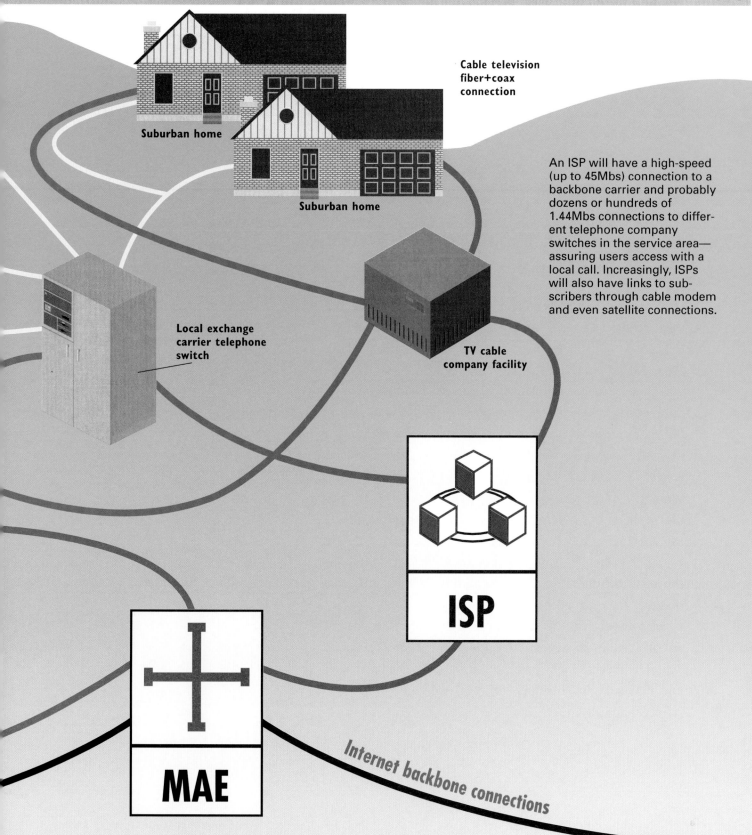

Cable television
fiber+coax
connection

Suburban home

Suburban home

An ISP will have a high-speed
(up to 45Mbs) connection to a
backbone carrier and probably
dozens or hundreds of
1.44Mbs connections to different telephone company
switches in the service area—
assuring users access with a
local call. Increasingly, ISPs
will also have links to subscribers through cable modem
and even satellite connections.

Local exchange
carrier telephone
switch

TV cable
company facility

ISP

MAE

Internet backbone connections

How an ISP Works

The Internet could logically be called the InterLAN because, in effect, it has become a network of local area networks. Even the resources of an Internet Service Provider are essentially a LAN. The type of operating system used by the various servers and the type of processors might vary with the size of the ISP, but the essential layout will be the same.

Incoming ISDN or analog calls from subscribers arrive at a remote access server. Data from subscribers connecting through cable modems arrives on a high speed line. If the calls come from a telephone company, they probably arrive on an ISDN primary rate line.

The first stop for the data is at an access control and billing server. This function might be built into a router, but more sophisticated systems use a separate server.

A DHCP server might also be an initial stop if the customer needs an IP address. It's common to have two DNS servers on-line because if one drops off or becomes bogged down, the entire system stops. We describe these terms more fully in the pages to come.

Subscribers typically see an initial screen, provided by the local Web server, with customized news and local information. They can pull e-mail from the ISP's e-mail server, newsgroup discussions from the newsgroup server, and frequently requested screens from the proxy server.

The ISP has high speed access, typically between 1.5 and 45Mbs, to one or more common Internet connection points. The subscribers share this access.

Authentication and billing server

Web server for local content

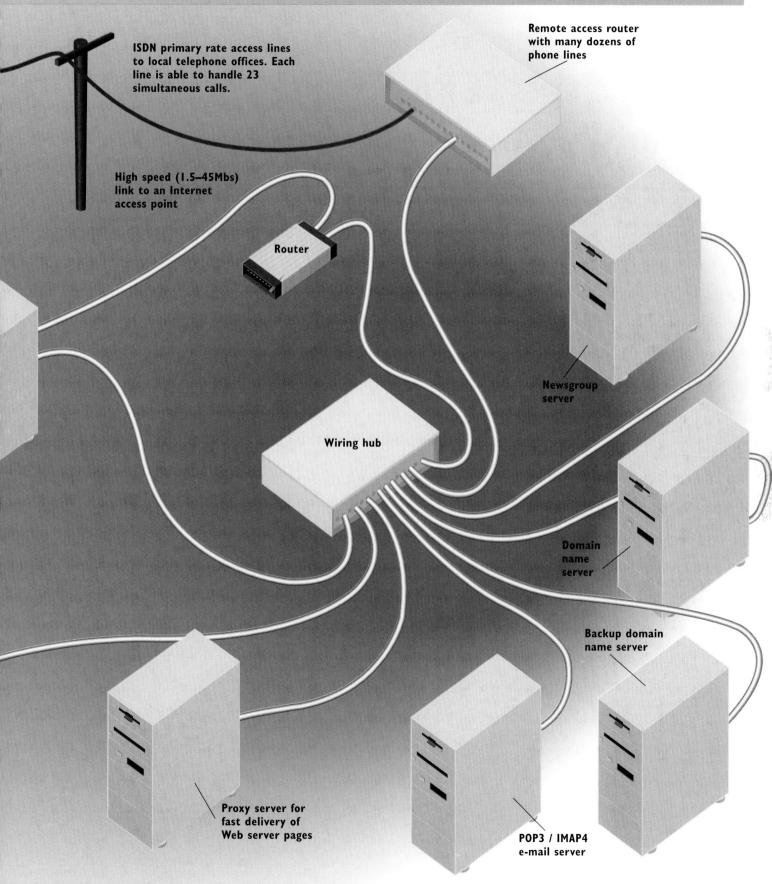

ISDN primary rate access lines to local telephone offices. Each line is able to handle 23 simultaneous calls.

Remote access router with many dozens of phone lines

High speed (1.5–45Mbs) link to an Internet access point

Router

Newsgroup server

Wiring hub

Domain name server

Backup domain name server

Proxy server for fast delivery of Web server pages

POP3 / IMAP4 e-mail server

How the TCP/IP Protocol Family Works

The TCP/IP family of protocols is a loose aggregation of standards that evolved from UNIX operating systems, from the evolution of the Internet, and from the actions to develop systems independent of any single manufacturer. The Internet Architecture Board (IAB) standardizes these protocols through several committees. The committees issue Requests for Comment (RFCs) and Standards (STD).

There are hundreds of RFCs and STDs, but the products on this chart are the most important for Internet activity. If you want more information, search for RFC2000, a general index, using any Internet search service.

The value of this architecture is that it promotes interoperability. Companies like IBM and Digital developed protocol families with equal capabilties, but they were largely proprietary. Products for the TCP/IP family were developed through cooperation among hundreds of companies.

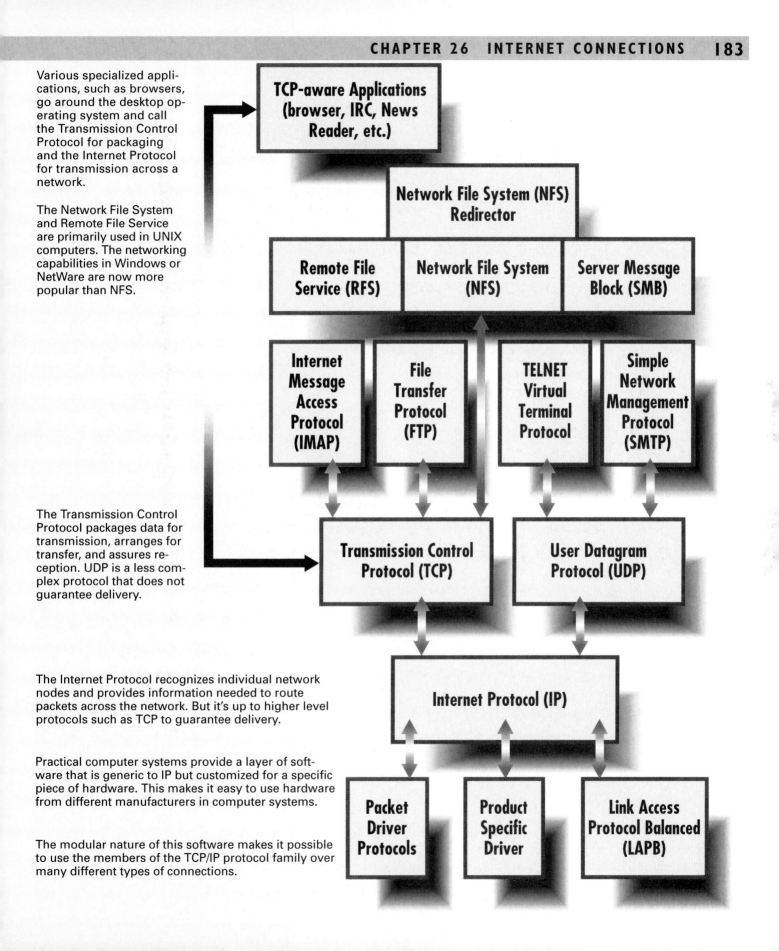

Various specialized applications, such as browsers, go around the desktop operating system and call the Transmission Control Protocol for packaging and the Internet Protocol for transmission across a network.

The Network File System and Remote File Service are primarily used in UNIX computers. The networking capabilities in Windows or NetWare are now more popular than NFS.

The Transmission Control Protocol packages data for transmission, arranges for transfer, and assures reception. UDP is a less complex protocol that does not guarantee delivery.

The Internet Protocol recognizes individual network nodes and provides information needed to route packets across the network. But it's up to higher level protocols such as TCP to guarantee delivery.

Practical computer systems provide a layer of software that is generic to IP but customized for a specific piece of hardware. This makes it easy to use hardware from different manufacturers in computer systems.

The modular nature of this software makes it possible to use the members of the TCP/IP protocol family over many different types of connections.

TCP-aware Applications (browser, IRC, News Reader, etc.)

Network File System (NFS) Redirector

Remote File Service (RFS)

Network File System (NFS)

Server Message Block (SMB)

Internet Message Access Protocol (IMAP)

File Transfer Protocol (FTP)

TELNET Virtual Terminal Protocol

Simple Network Management Protocol (SMTP)

Transmission Control Protocol (TCP)

User Datagram Protocol (UDP)

Internet Protocol (IP)

Packet Driver Protocols

Product Specific Driver

Link Access Protocol Balanced (LAPB)

How Domains and the Domain Name System Work

IP addressing works for computers and routers, but it's tough for humans to deal with 32-bit or 128-bit numbers. A naming system using a series of domains was developed for human use along with a system for mapping domain names to IP addresses. When you type in an address such as fred@company.com, you are kicking off a series of interchanges conducted by software within your computer and servers throughout your local network or the Internet.

There are more than 200 national or country top-level domains. There are also generic domains like .com for commercial users, .org for non-profit organizations, .gov for government entities, and .net for network service providers. Companies, organizations, and individuals can reserve sub-level domain names for a low annual fee.

The Domain Name System consists of servers throughout the Internet that maintain lists of nodes within a sub-domain and lists of other domain name servers. Governments and private organizations maintain "A" level Domain Name System servers with authoratative lists of all name system servers.

IP nodes typically contain the IP addresses of several local DNS servers. If the node requests correlation between a domain name and an IP address that the local DNS doesn't hold, it refers to an appropriate DNS for that sub-domain. If it doesn't have a DNS for the sub-domain, the DNS will refer to a higher level national server.

While this exchange of DNS information happens quickly and invisibly, it's critical to the efficient use of any IP network. Local DNS servers, provided either by a local network manager or an ISP, are important parts of a corporate intranet and the Internet.

DNS Step 4: Here's Fred's IP address

Internet connection

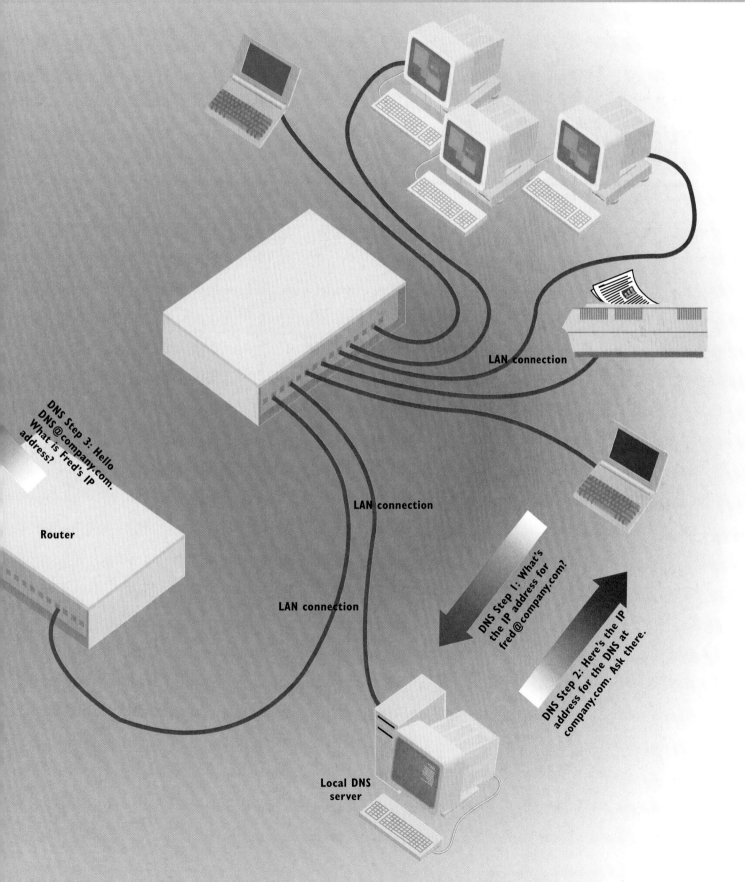

LAN connection

LAN connection

LAN connection

Router

DNS Step 3: Hello DNS@company.com. What is Fred's IP address?

Local DNS server

DNS Step 1: What's the IP address for fred@company.com?

DNS Step 2: Here's the IP address for the DNS at company.com. Ask there.

How DHCP and NAT save IP Addresses

There's a limited supply of IP addresses conforming to the Internet scheme. Two protocols, Dynamic Host Configuration (DHCP) and Network Address Translation (NAT), work in many networks to manage IP addresses and to reduce the need for conforming addresses.

DHCP assigns addresses to network devices on an as-requested basis. So, if a computer isn't turned on, it isn't occupying a valuable IP address. The address assignment typically expires after a set time and the device automatically renews with the server. If the address isn't renewed, it goes back into the queue. Some devices, such as printers and routers, have static assignments, but most client computers can have dynamic assignments.

The DHC server function is typically built into routers, although it might run in other devices such as file servers. If you have more than one DHC server in an extended network, they can coordinate their IP address assignments. DHC makes it easy to manage a block of IP addresses.

NAT reduces the need for IP addresses that are registered for use in the Internet. The NAT function, also typically built into routers, translates between one registered and conforming IP address assigned to the router and a subnetwork of unregistered addresses used on the LAN. NAT reduces the need for registered IP addresses.

An extension of the NAT idea is to use a less complex protocol, such as the Internet Packet Exchange (IPX), on the LAN and to all the gateway routers to completely re-package the data moving between the Internet and the LAN.

NAT: Packet Re-addressed to the Internet

NAT: Packet Re-addressed to the Internet

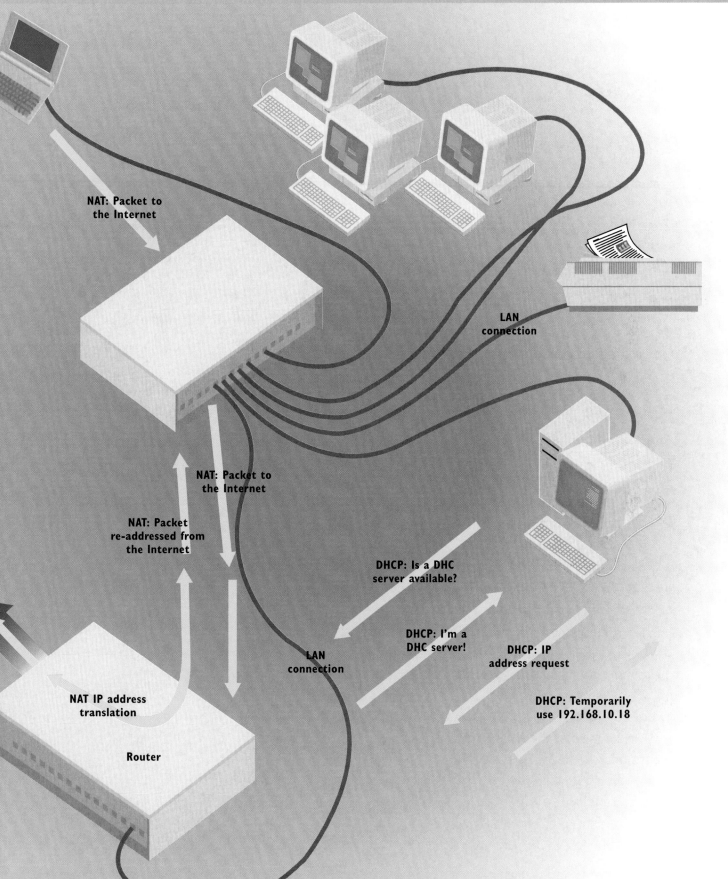

NAT: Packet to
the Internet

NAT: Packet to
the Internet

NAT: Packet
re-addressed from
the Internet

LAN
connection

LAN
connection

NAT IP address
translation

Router

DHCP: Is a DHC
server available?

DHCP: I'm a
DHC server!

DHCP: IP
address request

DHCP: Temporarily
use 192.168.10.18

How TCP and Denial of Service Attacks Work

The TCP-layer software packages data for transmission by IP. IP uses a technique called a *datagram*. As a datagram, the IP packet shoots into the network toward a specific destination without any way of ensuring its delivery. The TCP software uses accounting and persistence to provide assurance that, if it's possible, a packet will get through. Software conforming to TCP literally calls ahead to the destination to arrange reception for an incoming packet. The origination and destination computers agree on a control number for the incoming packet; the originating computer sends the packet, starts a clock, and goes on to other business.

Packing and tracking the data and making the best effort to deliver it to the end point are the important functions of TCP. However, this exchange creates its own network overhead. Another protocol, the User Datagram Protocol (UDP), does the packaging without the tracking. It's used for non-critical data transmissions such as broadcasts of management information and for applications that perform their own control over tracking and retransmission.

If all goes well during the TCP exchange, the TCP software at the destination sends an acknowledgement message (ACK) to the origination point using the control number. If the origination software doesn't get an ACK in sufficient time, it repeats the transmission. The origination point can adjust the elapsed time criteria based on previous experience with the destination.

Internet vandals try to use the TCP SYN process in what is termed a "denial of service" attack. They use special software to generate a stream of SYN messages that appear to come from various IP addresses. The victim of a SYN attack becomes overloaded and legitimate users are denied service. There are various countermeasures for these attacks, including patches that increase the capacity of the SYN data buffers. ISPs also have a responsibility to block originating traffic coming from one source wth wildly differing IP addresses.

The TCP process is another of the complex and invisible operations that you initiate every time you send files, e-mail, Web page requests, or other traffic across a TCP/IP network.

"SYN Attack" from across the Internet

SYN: Do you want this packet?

SYN: Do you want this packet?

SYN: Do you want this packet?

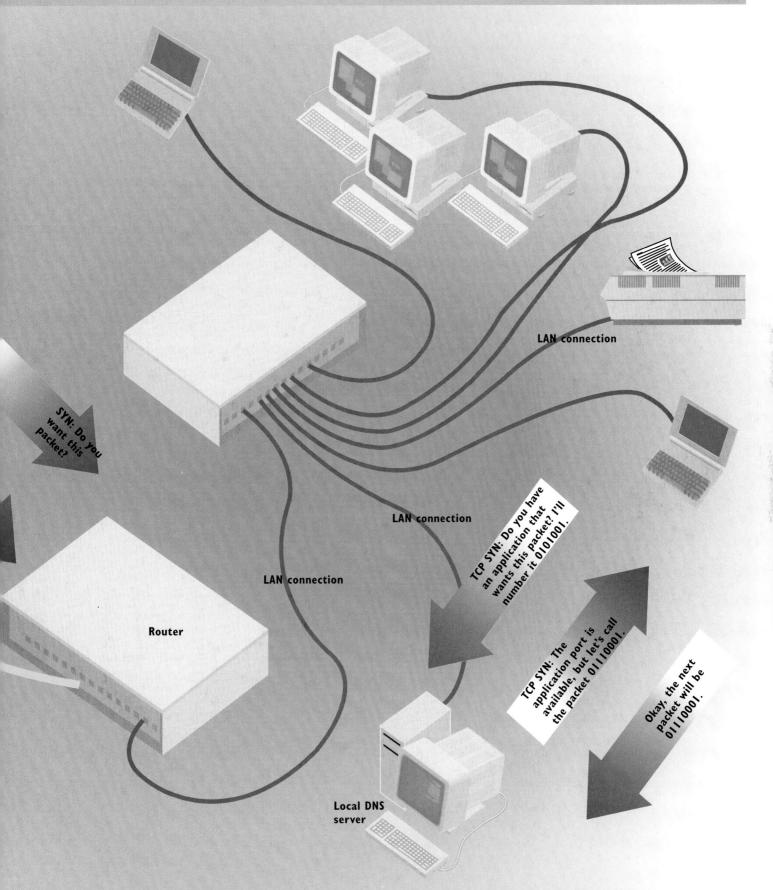

SYN: Do you want this packet?

LAN connection

LAN connection

LAN connection

Router

TCP SYN: Do you have an application that wants this packet? I'll number it 0101001.

TCP SYN: The application port is available, but let's call the packet 01110001.

Okay, the next packet will be 01110001.

Local DNS server

How IP Addressing Works

Every computer on any network needs an address. Some networks use an address assigned to each LAN adapter by its manufacturer. The Internet and IP-based LANs connected to the Internet use addresses assigned by an administrator. Every device on the Internet or on a corporate intranet—including printers, routers, managed hubs, and any other networked device—needs a unique address conforming to the Internet Protocol (IP) addressing scheme. This top-down scheme allows administrators to create and control their own subnetworks within the overall Internet.

The current addressing scheme, IP version 4, uses an address with 32 bits. One part of the address identifies the subnetwork and the other identifies the node on the subnet. The addresses are divided into three classes, A, B, and C, with different bit patterns shown in the table below. Each class allows for a different number of subnetworks and end nodes. The end node address space can be used to further subdivide a network.

The 126 blocks of Class A addresses have been allocated to governments and large institutions. Internet Service Providers have blocks of Class B or Class C addresses that they sub-allocate to customers. The number of available IP addresses is limited, so techniques such as Network Address Translation (NAT), described later in this chapter, are useful. A new addressing scheme, IP version 6, uses 128-bit addresses and can handle a huge number of subnets and nodes.

Address Class	Address Range	Number of subnets	Number of nodes
Class A: 7-bit network address field and a 24-bit node address field	001.XXX.XXX.XXX to 126.XXX.XXX.XXX	126	16,777,214
Class B: 14-bit network address field and a 16-bit node address field	128.001.XXX.XXX to 191.254.XXX.XXX	16,382	65,534
Class C: 21-bit network address field and an 8-bit node address field	192.000.001.XXX to 223.255.254.XXX	2,097,150	254

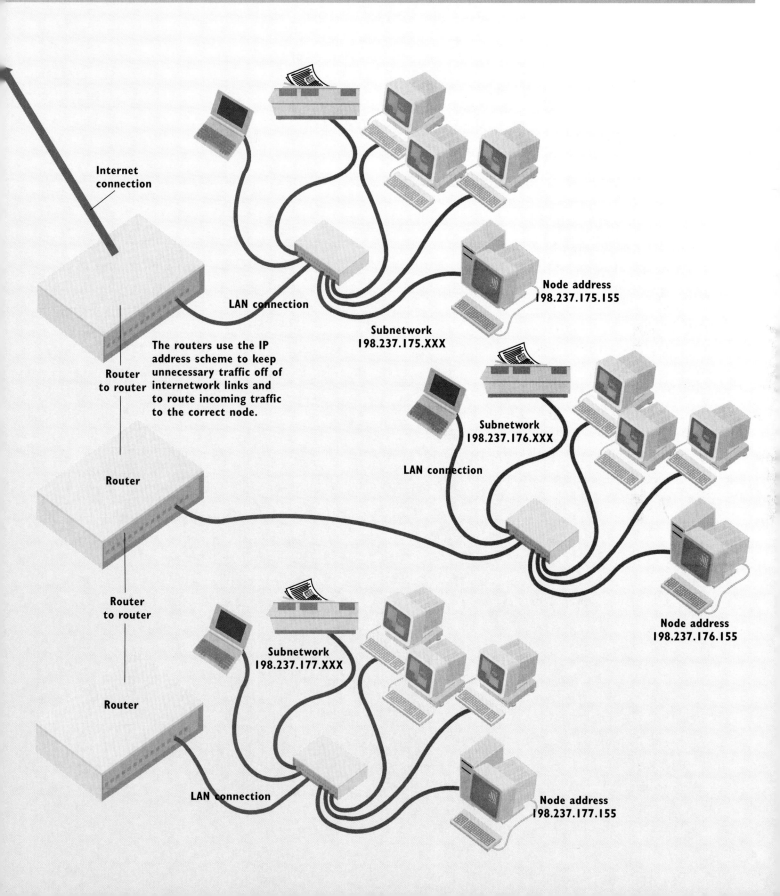

Internet connection

LAN connection

Router to router

The routers use the IP address scheme to keep unnecessary traffic off of internetwork links and to route incoming traffic to the correct node.

Router

Router to router

Router

Node address 198.237.175.155

Subnetwork 198.237.175.XXX

Subnetwork 198.237.176.XXX

LAN connection

Node address 198.237.176.155

Subnetwork 198.237.177.XXX

LAN connection

Node address 198.237.177.155

How the Web Server Works

A Web server can be part of the Internet, part of a corporate intranet, or simply a resource on a workgroup LAN. In each case, it works basically the same way.

A computer's browser sends a request encoded in the Hypertext Transfer Protocol (HTTP) to the Web server. The Web server sends a stream of Hypertext Markup Language (HTML) script, embedded with graphics and other scripts. The computer executes the script and recreates the screen.

Lotus, Microsoft, Attachmate, Digital, and other companies have or plan for automated links between Web servers and discussion/document databases.

Discussion and document databases

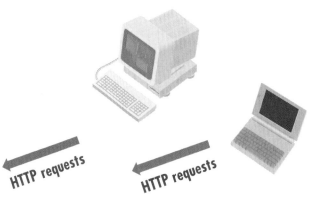

HTML screens

HTTP requests

HTTP requests

For most requests, the Web server will withdraw an HTML-formatted page from its own store or from a file server and broadcast it back to the requesting browser.

HTML screens

File server

Web servers typically conform to the Common Gateway Interface (CGI) application program interface (API). Programmers can write applications in the Perl or C++ languages that make SQL calls in response to browser requests.

Web server software

Sun's Java, Microsoft's OLE, Macromedia's Shockwave, and other products can interface with some browsers to create interactive applications socketed in the browser and working through the browser and Web server.

CGI/SQL application

SQL query and response

PC-based database server

Database processing tasks

Java, OLE, or Shockwave applications

How E-mail Works

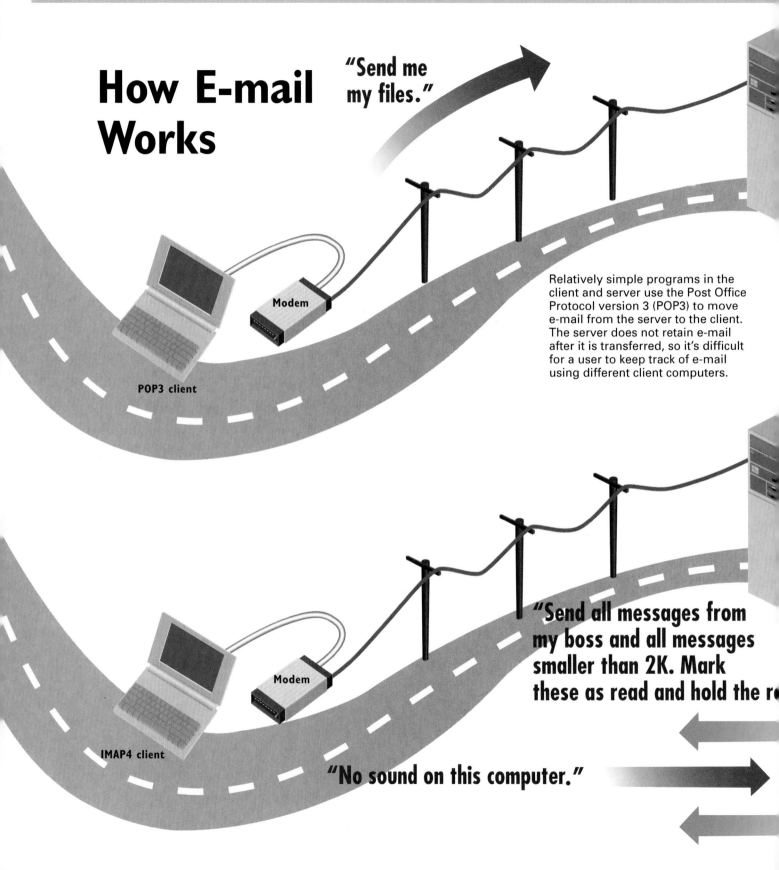

"Send me my files."

POP3 client

Relatively simple programs in the client and server use the Post Office Protocol version 3 (POP3) to move e-mail from the server to the client. The server does not retain e-mail after it is transferred, so it's difficult for a user to keep track of e-mail using different client computers.

IMAP4 client

"Send all messages from my boss and all messages smaller than 2K. Mark these as read and hold the re

"No sound on this computer."

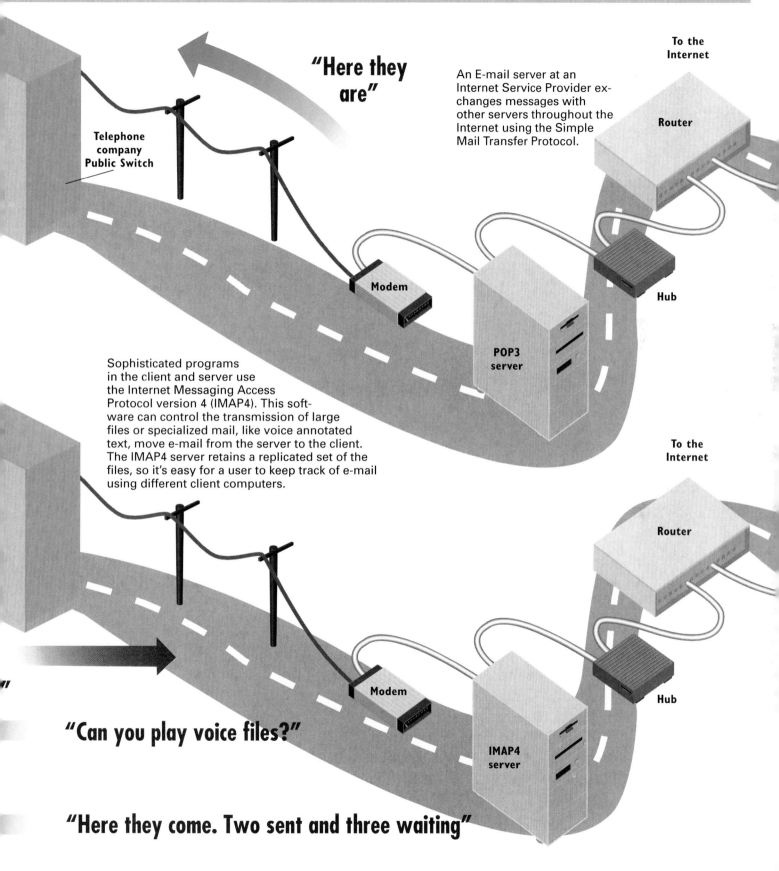

To the Internet

"Here they are"

An E-mail server at an Internet Service Provider exchanges messages with other servers throughout the Internet using the Simple Mail Transfer Protocol.

Router

Telephone company Public Switch

Modem

Hub

POP3 server

Sophisticated programs in the client and server use the Internet Messaging Access Protocol version 4 (IMAP4). This software can control the transmission of large files or specialized mail, like voice annotated text, move e-mail from the server to the client. The IMAP4 server retains a replicated set of the files, so it's easy for a user to keep track of e-mail using different client computers.

To the Internet

Router

Modem

Hub

"Can you play voice files?"

IMAP4 server

"Here they come. Two sent and three waiting"

How Virtual Private Networks Work

With its growing capacity and worldwide presence, the Internet has the potential to economically carry data between corporate local area networks. But moving sensitive corporate data across the the Internet opens potential problems with security and reliability. So several vendors, including Microsoft, U.S. Robotics, 3Com, and Cisco, developed techniques to improve the security and reliable delivery of corporate data moving across the Internet. The proprietary techniques include the Point-to-Point Tunneling Protocol (PPTP) and Layer 2 Forwarding Protocol (L2F). The companies eventually cooperated with the Internet Task Force to create a non-proprietary protocol called the Layer 2 Tunneling Protocol (L2TP).

All of these protocols generally work in the same way. Software in a router or server in each intercommunicating LAN encapsulates Internet-bound data in a special L2TP packet with encryption and accounting functions. The L2TP tunneling packet is wrapped in a standard IP packet for transmission across the Internet. At the destination, the L2TP-compliant router or server strips off the packaging and sends it out across the local network.

The action of software in each LAN creates one form of what is called a Virtual Private Network (VPN) through the Internet. Instead of using your own software, you can also get a VPN subscription from Internet carriers. Many carriers offer subscription VPN services that include features such as remote access through the Internet.

A VPN can significantly reduce the cost of corporate LAN interconnections and provide great flexibility, but even with the help of tunneling, reliability isn't assured.

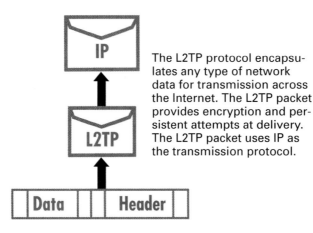

The L2TP protocol encapsulates any type of network data for transmission across the Internet. The L2TP packet provides encryption and persistent attempts at delivery. The L2TP packet uses IP as the transmission protocol.

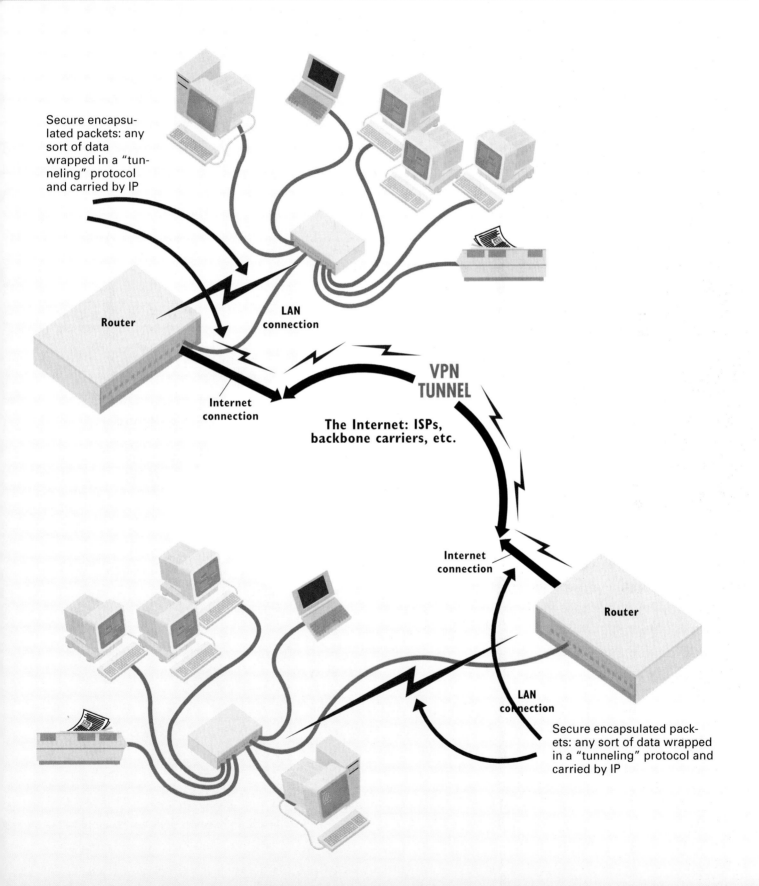

Secure encapsulated packets: any sort of data wrapped in a "tunneling" protocol and carried by IP

Router

LAN connection

Internet connection

VPN TUNNEL

The Internet: ISPs, backbone carriers, etc.

Internet connection

Router

LAN connection

Secure encapsulated packets: any sort of data wrapped in a "tunneling" protocol and carried by IP

How Remote Access Works Across the Internet

The Internet can play an important part in meeting remote access needs. Overall, there are four approaches to creating a remote access capability. Three approaches involve doing more or less of your own system integration. One approach involves subscribing to a complete service.

You can create your own remote access solution using an existing NetWare or Windows NT server, special remote access server software from Novell or Microsoft, and either internal or external communications devices. Callers dial through the public telephone system using either ISDN or analog modems. Today, the telephone company will typically deliver all incoming calls to your remote access server over digital ISDN lines. This approach has the advantage of low initial cost and a monthly cost based on usage.

You can pay a little more and buy a turn-key remote access server from one of a dozen vendors. Otherwise the system is the same as rolling your own access server. You'll have fewer setup problems, but greater initial cost and finite expansion capabilities.

You can significantly reduce communications costs by setting up your own tunneling servers or routers to create virtual private network VPN connections across the Internet. Client computers run special tunneling software, call any ISP for Internet access, and then connect to your hardware. The data is encrypted and the circuit has good reliability. This approach has a significant up-front cost, but low recurring costs.

If you want to avoid all technical challenges, you can subscribe to a remote access service. This type of service, typically provided by an ISP, also uses virtual private networking and tunneling, but the ISP provides and maintains all the equipment. Depending on the connection needs, the calls might or might not traverse the Internet. This approach offers a level cost. You have good flexibility and the ability to expand service, but it can be costly to make changes to contracted services.

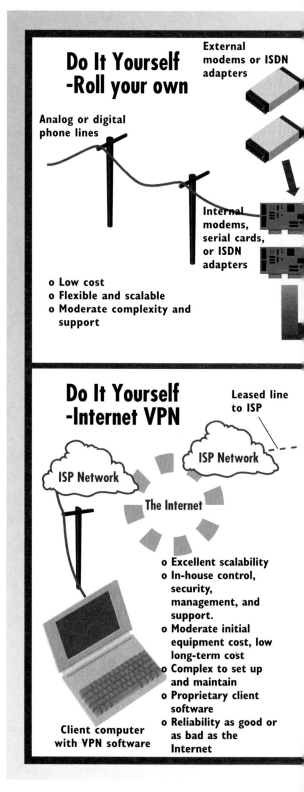

Do It Yourself -Roll your own

External modems or ISDN adapters

Analog or digital phone lines

Internal modems, serial cards, or ISDN adapters

- o Low cost
- o Flexible and scalable
- o Moderate complexity and support

Do It Yourself -Internet VPN

Leased line to ISP

ISP Network

ISP Network

The Internet

- o Excellent scalability
- o In-house control, security, management, and support.
- o Moderate initial equipment cost, low long-term cost
- o Complex to set up and maintain
- o Proprietary client software
- o Reliability as good or as bad as the Internet

Client computer with VPN software

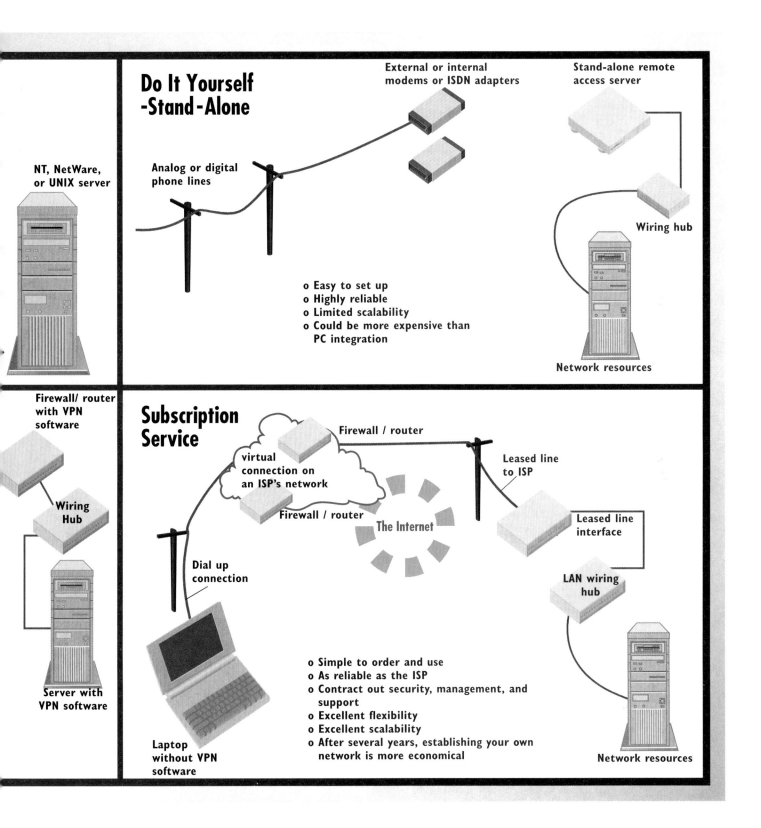

Do It Yourself -Stand-Alone

External or internal modems or ISDN adapters

Stand-alone remote access server

NT, NetWare, or UNIX server

Analog or digital phone lines

Wiring hub

o Easy to set up
o Highly reliable
o Limited scalability
o Could be more expensive than PC integration

Network resources

Subscription Service

Firewall/ router with VPN software

Wiring Hub

Server with VPN software

virtual connection on an ISP's network

Firewall / router

Firewall / router

The Internet

Leased line to ISP

Leased line interface

LAN wiring hub

Dial up connection

Laptop without VPN software

o Simple to order and use
o As reliable as the ISP
o Contract out security, management, and support
o Excellent flexibility
o Excellent scalability
o After several years, establishing your own network is more economical

Network resources

How Firewall LAN Connections Work

The purpose of a firewall is to securely separate the Internet and other external networks from your corporate LAN. Firewalls use several different techniques to inspect the content, not just the destination, of incoming packets to determine if they warrant access.

A firewall might be a piece of turn-key hardware or it might be a function included in software running on a special server. Firewall software is available for a variety of operating systems.

The best configuration for the firewall service is to segment the network into at least three parts. The Internet connection enters the firewall on a separate LAN adapter. This gives the firewall total control over the routing of those packets. The firewall server can similarly host another LAN adapter for connections to other corporate LANs. The firewall server and those connections are referred to as the perimeter LAN. A third LAN adapter links the firewall to the protected LAN.

A network administrator can configure the firewall to deny access to many kinds of data, such as FTP file transfers. This improves the security of the system and removes possible holes in the firewall.

In this example, a remote access router gives callers access to the LAN behind the firewall. This assumes that the remote access system has an internal security system. These remote access servers typically read security data from the central file system.

Behind the firewall, the corporate intranet looks a lot like an ISP. However, many functions that an ISP might set up on separate servers, like DHCP and DNS, can be combined in an intranet.

Router connection

Wiring hub

Link to an ISP

Router with high-speed Internet access

Web server for corporate content

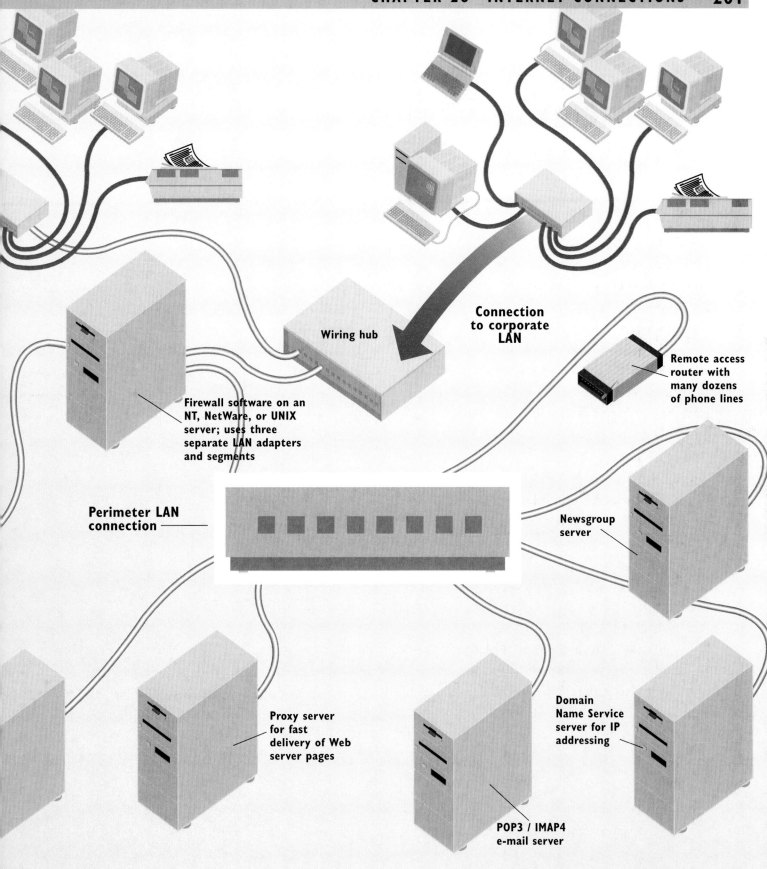

Connection
to corporate
LAN

Wiring hub

Remote access
router with
many dozens
of phone lines

Firewall software on an
NT, NetWare, or UNIX
server; uses three
separate LAN adapters
and segments

Perimeter LAN
connection

Newsgroup
server

Domain
Name Service
server for IP
addressing

Proxy server
for fast
delivery of Web
server pages

POP3 / IMAP4
e-mail server

Index